The Harrison House Vision

Proclaiming the truth and the power

Of the Gospel of Jesus Christ

With excellence;

Challenging Christians to

Live victoriously,

Grow spiritually,

Know God intimately.

INNOVATION

By

Drs. Bill & Anne Moore

Harrison House
Tulsa, OK

Scripture quotations marked NKJV are taken from the *New King James Version®*. Copyright © 1982 by Thomas Nelson, Inc. Used by permission. All rights reserved.

Scripture quotations marked NLT are taken from the *Holy Bible, New Living Translation*, copyright © 1996, 2004, 2007 by Tyndale House Foundation. Used by permission of Tyndale House Publishers, Inc., Carol Stream, Illinois 60188. All rights reserved.

Scripture quotations marked KJV are taken from the *King James Version* of the Bible.

Scripture quotations marked TEV are taken from the *Good News Translation in Today's English Version*- Second Edition. Copyright © 1992 by American Bible Society. Used by permission.

Scripture quotations marked MSG are taken from *The Message*. Copyright © 1993, 1994, 1995, 1996, 2000, 2001, 2002. Used by permission of NavPress Publishing Group.

Scripture quotations marked TLB are taken from *The Living Bible*. Copyright © 1971, 1997 by Tyndale House Publishers, Inc. Used by permission. All rights reserved.

Scripture quotations marked NIV are taken from *The Holy Bible, New International Version®*, NIV® Copyright © 1973, 1978, 1984, 2011 by Biblica, Inc.® Used by permission. All rights reserved worldwide.

Scripture quotations marked AMP are taken from the *Amplified® Bible*, Copyright © 1954, 1958, 1962, 1964, 1965, 1987 by The Lockman Foundation. Used by permission. (www.Lockman.org)

Scripture quotations marked ESV are taken from *The Holy Bible, English Standard Version®* (ESV®), copyright © 2001 by Crossway, a publishing ministry of Good News Publishers. Used by permission. All rights reserved.

17 16 15 14   10 9 8 7 6 5 4 3 2 1

Innovation
ISBN 978-160683-869-3
Copyright © 2014 by Bill Moore

Published by Harrison House Publishers

Printed in the United States of America. All rights reserved under International Copyright Law. Contents and/or cover may not be reproduced in whole or in part in any form without the express written consent of the Publisher.

Table of Contents

Introduction

Chapter 1   Hardwired for Creativity 1

Chapter 2   If Your Brook's Dried Up, Create a New Stream ... 9

Chapter 3   An Unconventional Approach 17

Chapter 4   Crime Scene 27

Chapter 5   Two Trees 39

Chapter 6   God's Justice System 47

Chapter 7   The Government of God 55

Chapter 8   Digging Ditches 67

Chapter 9   Visions and Dreams 77

Chapter 10   Visions and Dreams - Part 2 87

Chapter 11   Corporate Vision 95

Chapter 12   To My Haters and Underestimators 105

Chapter 13   A Work in Progress 113

Chapter 14   Responding to Critics 119

Chapter 15   Open Heavens 131

Chapter 16   Favor for the Moment 143

Chapter 17   Favor the Elevator 153

Chapter 18   Honor Brings Favor.. 163

Introduction

So many people in our world are in a very difficult place. With the looming threat of world economic collapse, the rule of demented dictators, and the threat of nuclear and chemical weapons, the world at large is struggling for perspective. Innovation is God's answer to our crisis. Innovation reveals what we do not see; it helps us see what is so clear to Divinity but so vague to humanity. Innovation gives us the winning edge; it is the missing link that makes a huge difference in our final outcome.

God has always engineered a way of escape for His people - a prison for Joseph, a staff for Moses, a trumpet for Joshua, a jawbone for Samson, a widow woman and her son for Elijah, a field of barley for Ruth, a boy's lunch for the disciples, Peter's boat for Jesus' sermon. Innovation is a change in the thought process; the useful application of new inventions or discoveries to get things done. It may refer to an incremental emergence or radical revolutionary changes in thinking, products, processes or organizations. Innovators refresh; they constantly recreate themselves in their organization because yesterday's cutting edge is today's dull and antiquated.

It has been said that everything we need is in our hand. God uses the things we already have to create the future we want. There are miracles of creativity and miracles of conversion. Think about the miracles Jesus performed when He walked the earth. He performed miracles of creativity and conversion that brought

Him glory and fulfilled His purpose in the earth using ordinary things found in our sinful lives. When money was needed, Christ pointed out the coin in the fish's mouth. He was showing us that we must remain innovative in spirit. A donkey in the street and a ram in the thicket all point toward a God who invites us to live in His creative dimension.

It's been said that if all you have is a hammer, everything looks like a nail. In this book on innovation, you will discover that there are a multitude of tools God has placed in your toolbox. He has placed you in a world of possibilities and potential. Learn to wake up every day and declare, "The Creator lives in me to release His plan and purpose through me. The best has not yet been seen." Allow God to put big dreams in your heart, dreams that are bigger than what you would have ever dared imagine yourself. As Erwin McMannis said, "God speaks to us in a dream, so we can live the life of our dreams."

Chapter One

Hardwired for Creativity

Albert Einstein once said, "The world as we created it is a result of our thinking. It cannot be changed without changing our thinking." Einstein clashed with educational authorities as a child, which is perhaps what led him to write that the spirit of learning and creative thought is often lost in strict rote and perspective teaching. He later went on to challenge conventional wisdom and in doing so, redefined many of the sacred scientific theories that had for so long been embraced. His great intellectual achievements and originality have made the name Einstein synonymous with genius.

I want to begin this first chapter with some fresh fuel for creative thinkers. I would love for you to start every day with this faith declaration: "The Creator is in me today and He is opening the eyes of my understanding, giving me insight into His purpose and plan for my life." Innovation is the creation of a better or more effective product, process or service through optimized creativity. We understand from Scripture that it is the will of God to optimize creativity in our lives. Ephesians 1:19 says, "And what is the exceeding greatness of His power toward us who believe, according to the working of His mighty power" (NKJV).

God wants to give us a revelation daily of how much He has vested in our lives. There is tremendous power and grace available to each and every one of us; we need only learn to make daily withdrawals on His divine creativity. The Word of God says in Nehemiah 9:20, "You also gave Your good Spirit to instruct them, and did not withhold Your manna from their mouth, and gave them water for their thirst" (NKJV). As He has done since the outset, God provides for every need of His children.

It is easy to see the correlation between the leadership of God in our lives and the provision that God has planned for our lives. Many people seek God's hand without seeking God's heart. The key to living a life filled with the inspiration of the Almighty, with His divine creativity and innovation, is to seek God's heart. He said in Scripture that He gives His good Spirit to instruct us, and because He instructs us from within, we're able to lay hold of the blessings - the manna, the provision or the water as the scripture says - for our thirst. The Spirit will lead you to a place of greater blessing. As you learn to listen, rely and cling to Him, the Holy Spirit within you will lead you to a place of great advantage and innovation in this life.

What a difference a day can make. I woke up one morning and was listening to the news about the devastating tornadoes that had moved through the Tuscaloosa, Alabama, area. Within just a moment of hearing the news, my phone began to sound Twitter alerts, as tweets from various large ministries detailed efforts that were already underway to send food and clothes and necessary supplies for the victims of these terrible tornadoes. As I rose out of bed, I thought in my heart, *Lord, I wish our ministry could make a difference like these larger ministries. Lord, I want to have an impact on those lives and families in the Tuscaloosa area.* I just kind of breathed these thoughts to the Lord, having been somewhat provoked through the tweets of others mentioning their efforts and abilities to do something in the wake of this terrible tragedy.

As I got to the church office around 9:30 that morning, my phone rang. The first call that came in that day was from the director of the Parks and Recreation department of our city. He said, "Pastor, the Lord has laid it on my heart to send provisions to Alabama. Is there anything we can do?" Within the scope of about five minutes, we had procured a large trailer and this brother volunteered to take it to the mall and set it up as a collection site. By noon, we were collecting items to benefit the people of Alabama. The Lord heard my request – truly, He probably put the desire to help there - and as the Word said, He gave His good Spirit to instruct me. The Lord provided the manna, the water and the blessing as a result of our desire to serve others.

Well, I thought the procurement of the large trailer and the collection of goods that was underway was great, but God always does exceedingly abundantly above all we can ask or think. What starts out in a moment of an innovative thought can end up divinely transforming your entire life. Our church had been praying about engaging in more outreach and street ministry. That afternoon at about 1:30, a man showed up at the church and said, "Pastor, I want

Innovation

to help serve the Lord and pass out tracts and flyers. I want to reach out to those in our area to bring them to Christ." I prayed with this man and he immediately began to expand the outreach ministry of LivingWay Family Church. Not more than an hour after meeting with that man, one of the largest radio stations in our area called and said that they wanted to partner with our church to give over 3,000 backpacks away at a Back to School outreach that fall. God had made another divine connection, but He wasn't through yet!

I kept thinking how incredible it was that in one day, my thoughts combined with God's innovative ability blessed and expanded the kingdom of God. From the man contacting me with a burden to collect clothes for tornado victims in Alabama to the brother who showed up wanting to work in the outreach ministry of the church to the radio station that called and decided to partner with us to reach boys and girls through the Back to School program, God had given so many big gifts that day. Not long after, I was praying at another community function I had been invited to attend. That night, God connected me with yet a fourth individual whose homeless ministry is now feeding over 150 every Sunday morning. Again, I witnessed a divine connection. What a difference a day can make!

Sometimes God uses our desires that He has planted inside of us to innovate His deliverance. Psalm 37:4 says, "Delight yourself also in the Lord, and He shall give you the desires of your heart" (NKJV). God can place divine desires in our hearts to lead us to a place of breakthrough and blessing that we have never seen, the likes of which we've never experienced in our lives. Pastor Rick Warren says we are all hardwired by God for creativity. It's in our DNA, it's in our spirit, placed there by God that we might be creative. The Creator lives in us - the One who created the heavens and the earth, the One who threw the stars into their fiery sockets, the One who conceived all that we can see and all that we know. That same God lives on the inside of us. What uncanny ability we would have if only we would learn to apply Ephesians 1:19, if only we would understand "what is the exceeding greatness of His power toward us who believe, according to the working of His mighty power."

I believe God's creative power is working in you today as you believe Him, as you release your faith for the needs in your life. I believe God is working in you in a mighty way, and He is giving you a revelation of the exceeding power that He has made available to you. But it troubles my heart today to see so many of God's people miss His timing in their lives. They miss the thing that God wants to do in and through them at just the right time.

I want us to look in the Old Testament at 1 Kings 17. As we join this story, we see the prophet Elijah in the middle of a personal transition. He has a choice to make: stay in a dry creek bed and think about the streams of yesterday or somehow catch the next wave that he so desperately needs if he is to survive. Elijah understood the need to move with God, the need to experience transition. Elijah understood seasons of blessing in his life. A season, by definition, is a moment. A season is not "all the time." Many times when the brook dries up, God's people are not perceptive enough to discern that the dried up brook signals the end of a season. They cannot discern that a certain season of blessing, a certain season of a

Innovation

provision is over. God never wants His people to lack provision. He never wants His people to lack direction, which is why He provides continual direction. The key is in learning to perceive that direction. There's a need for us to learn how to create flow where there is no flow by responding to His good Spirit within us. That is living in the land of innovation.

Consider this account from 1 Kings 17:2-6: "Then the word of the LORD came to him, saying, 'Get away from here and turn eastward, and hide by the Brook Cherith, which flows into the Jordan. And it will be that you shall drink from the brook, and I have commanded the ravens to feed you there.' So he went and did according to the word of the LORD, for he went and stayed by the Brook Cherith, which flows into the Jordan. The ravens brought him bread and meat in the morning, and bread and meat in the evening; and he drank from the brook" (NKJV).

We must understand that our response to God must constantly be developing. Our ability to respond, our ability to discern between a season that is flourishing and a season that is changing is key to staying prosperous, to staying blessed, to staying on the cutting edge whether in ministry, business, industry, finance or family. Discerning the season is key. It is easy to get comfortable in a season when bread and meat are provided, when morning and evening you see the hand of God sustain you supernaturally. But we have to be alert to what God is doing not only right now, but also in our future because God wants to give us a vision of the future.

Hardwired for Creativity

The account of Elijah continues in 1 Kings 17:7-9: "And it happened after a while that the brook dried up, because there had been no rain in the land. Then the word of the Lord came to him, saying, 'Arise, go to Zarephath, which belongs to Sidon, and dwell there. See, I have commanded a widow there to provide for you'" (NKJV).

Notice the words of the Lord found in verse number 8, "Then the word of the Lord came to him, saying, 'Arise, go to Zarephath, which belongs to Sidon, and dwell there. See, I have commanded a widow there to provide for you'" (NKJV). Elijah had to make the move before he could see the provision. So many of God's people want to see the provision before they make the move. The word given to Elijah was rise and go, I'm taking you to a new place. That's innovation, that's creativity. God was saying to Elijah, "I'm taking you to a place that you've never seen before, but if you'll trust Me in that place, you'll see My hand, you'll see provision." A new season was developing in Elijah's life, and his success in that season was contingent upon him hearing from God and receiving that Spirit of innovation.

God wants to open a new door. God wants to bless you in a new way. He wants to open new revenue streams in your life, to release the Spirit of innovation in you. Our God is innovative, and He wants you to be an innovator as well.

Innovation

Chapter Two

If Your Brook's Dried Up, Create a New Stream

First Kings 17:7 says, "And it happened after a while that the brook dried up…" (NKJV). Time has a way of drying up the brook. I've discovered in my life that God will allow a brook to dry up to get me on my knees, to get me seeking Him more diligently, to get me praying more passionately because the just shall live by faith. God requires us to trust Him no matter what and to trust Him in every season. If the brook in your life has dried up, now is the time to seek the Lord diligently.

When your brook has dried up, there are three key components to creating a new stream that brims with excitement and provision. Number one, we must have a consuming focus. Number two, we must possess risk-taking faith. Number three, we must employ an unconventional approach.

Recent statistics show that people who live to age 100 are able to maneuver through the changes in their life. People who enjoy longevity are able to respond to the twists and turns that life sends their way. We've seen this type of thing happen in the entertainment industry with individuals like Robert Downey Jr., whose career was all but washed up but who, through personal growth and determination, rebounded and reinvented himself. We see the same principle in play in great entertainers like Tina Turner. In her latter years, she is still relevant and prospering in her career because she learned how to reinvent herself and stay fresh.

The word of the Lord came to Elijah telling him to arise and go. It was time for Elijah to move beyond yesterday's instruction into a new area. Innovation builds the bridge that spans the gap between the past and the future God has promised. Innovation is God's way of getting us from here to there.

In Genesis 28:15, God told Jacob, "I will not leave you until I have done what I have promised you" (NKJV). God has made promises about our future, and He will stand with us until those promises are fulfilled. Joseph realized that God's people would not live in Egypt forever but would one day possess the land promised to Abraham. This is why he made the Israelites promise that they would carry his bones up from that place when they left (Genesis 50:24-25). That's a revelation of the faithfulness of God. Joseph knew that what God promised, God would fulfill.

What has God vested in you? What word has He given you about your life? What gift has He given you? Many times people despair because things do not come to pass in the time in which they desire them to come to pass, but yet God is saying, "I'm standing with you because I have a vested interest in your life. I'm going to make sure My plans for your life are fully accomplished before your days on the earth are done."

As we travel through life we may start out in one direction, but we will eventually need innovation to help us maneuver through the difficult places and changes of life. God has promised to provide the innovative spirit we so desperately need. Second Peter 1:2-4 declares, "Grace and peace be multiplied to you in the knowledge of God and of Jesus our Lord, as His divine power has given to us all things that pertain to life and godliness, through the knowledge of Him who called us by glory and virtue, by which have been given to us exceedingly great and precious promises, that through these you may be partakers of the divine nature, having escaped the corruption that is in the world through lust" (NKJV).

We've been given great and precious promises. God is standing by us. He is standing by you even in the difficult places, to fulfill the promise that He made to you. These precious promises cause us to partake – to take portions - of God's divine nature which enables us to escape the corruption that is in the world. We can avoid many of life's pitfalls through the wisdom that God has given us. That's the spirit of innovation. God's Spirit of creativity working in us can guide us around the pitfalls of life.

The Word of the Lord tells us in Daniel chapter 1 verse 20 that Daniel and the three Hebrews had ten times more wisdom than all the others in the land. They are real-life examples of the spirit of innovation in action. The spirit of innovation they possessed kept them from partaking of the king's food and drink, which kept them healthy and their minds clear. God has promised us in 2 Peter 1:2-4 that He will do the same for us. He declares that we will escape the corruption that is in the world, we'll escape the pitfalls as we adhere to His promises and as we remember His Word. We are guided by the Word. This enables us to change, maneuver, and adjust so as

Innovation

not to be caught in a dry brook season. We need not be stuck in a dry river bed if we are able to transition as we hear the Word of the Lord saying, "I've provided another place that will sustain you."

The spirit of innovation may require us to move and act and respond. It may require a change in our geographical location or the way we do things. It is important to note that in the original Greek, the words "moment" and "movement" are synonymous. How appropriate that is. It is so important for each and every one of us to understand the moment we are living in and to know how to move within that moment, how to innovate in that moment so that we continue moving forward and do not get stuck in a dry brook season. We move in the right direction as we conceive in our hearts the thing God has promised.

Consider this passage from Exodus 14:13-16: "And Moses said to the people, 'Do not be afraid. Stand still, and see the salvation of the Lord, which He will accomplish for you today. For the Egyptians whom you see today, you shall see again no more forever. The Lord will fight for you, and you shall hold your peace.' And the Lord said to Moses, 'Why do you cry to Me? Tell the children of Israel to go forward. But lift up your rod, and stretch out your hand over the sea and divide it. And the children of Israel shall go on dry ground through the midst of the sea'" (NKJV).

Notice that there was instruction tied to the blessing. God told Moses, "You've prayed. Now it is time to act. Quit praying. Get moving. Stretch out your rod." So many reading this book are in a dry season. Many are in a dry season in their relationships with friends and family. Many are in a dry season in their careers; it seems advancement just will not come. Over the last several years, many have experienced a dry season economically. But God has a word for you that will provide the needed innovation in your life to bring you to a place of greater blessing. His instructions for you are to quit praying – you've prayed long enough - get moving now and stretch out your rod.

Notice that God called for Moses to take an unconventional approach. What practical good would you expect to come from a man stretching a rod out over the sea? How would that act move a sea? But God was innovating through Moses to bring about deliverance for His people. That's what God does for us, as well. He orchestrates through our innovation, transformation and deliverance in our lives.

In order for the people of God to be delivered, they would have to respond to the voice of the Lord. They would have to respond to God's Spirit of innovation in order to see their deliverance. If you don't know the rest of the story, let me tell you that the people did act on the instruction of God and God gave them passage through the sea. Just as He promised them, they saw those enemies no more when they acted on the instruction of the Lord.

I believe the lessons we can take from this story of the children of Israel are critical for somebody reading this book today. You are facing enemies of pain, enemies of fear, enemies of regret, enemies of sickness, enemies at home, enemies at work, enemies who work against what God has called you to do for His kingdom. But God wants you to know that if you will be led by His Spirit of creativity, He will cause your enemies to disappear. He will

Innovation

bring opportunities to your door and will help you overcome your obstacles. He'll do that for you. Just as with the children of Israel, God's work of innovation in your life and your response to God in obedience will open the sea before you.

Let's return to the story of Elijah found in 1 Kings 17.

When last we saw Elijah, he was transitioning. The brook had dried up. His former source of blessing had ceased to be, but God was still his ultimate source of provision. God, who is *El Shaddai* and *Jehovah Jireh*, had not abandoned Elijah. Elijah needed only to look to Him and be blessed. But Elijah had to be in that place where he could be blessed. He had to get in the right realm. He had to position himself so that he could be blessed by God. Only in his obedience could the favor of God could find him.

Let's rejoin Elijah's story in 1 Kings 17:10-15:

"So he arose and went to Zarephath. And when he came to the gate of the city, indeed a widow was there gathering sticks. And he called to her and said, 'Please bring me a little water in a cup, that I may drink.' And as she was going to get it, he called to her and said, 'Please bring me a morsel of bread in your hand.'

"So she said, 'As the Lord your God lives, I do not have bread, only a handful of flour in a bin, and a little oil in a jar; and see, I am gathering a couple of sticks that I may go in and prepare it for myself and my son, that we may eat it, and die.'

"And Elijah said to her, 'Do not fear; go and do as you have said, but make me a small cake from it first, and bring it to me;

and afterward make some for yourself and your son. For thus says the Lord God of Israel: "The bin of flour shall not be used up, nor shall the jar of oil run dry, until the day the Lord sends rain on the earth."'

"So she went away and did according to the word of Elijah; and she and he and her household ate for many days." (NKJV)

Do not miss the message of verse 15 – the woman went away and did as the Lord had instructed her through His prophet Elijah. This dear woman received a solution to her dilemma through her obedience. Sometimes when God gives us the opportunity to give, the opportunity to release something back to Him by giving to our local church or to a ministry or some worthwhile cause, sometimes we fail to see God in that opportunity. But our act of obedience in releasing our seed is part of God's innovative process to bring us into a greater realm of blessing. When God innovates, He elevates. It is His desire to take your life to a higher place of favor. It is His desire to bring you into a land that flows with milk and honey, but you can only get there through obedience.

Notice Elijah gave specific instructions to the woman. God will do the same for us, and it is important that we follow His specific instructions. Elijah instructed the woman to make a cake for him first and bring it to him and afterward, she was to make a cake for herself and her son. He presented an unconventional solution to the problem that was facing that woman and her son. Because the woman was willing to step out in faith and obey the word of the Lord given through His servant Elijah, she was delivered by that word from her last day to her best day.

Innovation

I heard a story of a couple that loved to take hikes. Once when they were hiking in the mountains of California, they came across a field of mushrooms. They loved to eat mushrooms, so they collected all they could carry and brought the mushrooms back to their house. That night, they invited some friends over and prepared all kinds of different dishes that included mushrooms. After they'd finished eating they had leftovers, so they gave some to their cat and went on about the evening fellowshipping and talking with one another. At one point in the evening, they looked over and saw their cat foaming at the mouth and going into convulsions in the corner. They realized something was desperately wrong, so they called their veterinarian. The veterinarian said, "I'm sure that you have not eaten good mushrooms, but poisonous toadstools. It's important for you to get to the hospital and have your stomachs pumped at once."

The couple and their friends rushed out to the hospital and had their stomachs pumped. It was a terrible ordeal. When they finally returned to the house, they expected to find their cat deceased in the corner, but instead they found that the cat had given birth to a litter of kittens. They had misinterpreted birth pains as death pains.

How many times have we made the same mistake by acting in haste and misinterpreting the instructions we receive from God? God's message to us is clear; we need only listen attentively and obey. We have to listen carefully, understanding that one word from God can reinvent our lives and innovate a deliverance, turning a dry brook into a flowing stream once again.

Chapter Three
An Unconventional Approach

As believers in Christ, we need to rely on God's instructional voice. The instructional voice of God leads us, just like it did Elijah, to a new place of greater abundance. In 1 Kings 17:8, the word of the Lord came to Elijah saying, "Arise and go." Each and every one of us either has had or will have an "arise and go" moment in our spirit. When you have an "arise and go" moment, you will see God reveal the full measure of His prosperity and His plan for your life. Innovation is the bridge between the past and the future God has promised; it is the path to take you from living in the land of lack to living in the land of abundance that God has in store for each and every one of His children.

In Genesis 28:15, God told Jacob, "I will stand with you until My promise is fulfilled" (my paraphrase). We have to know that God is working to accomplish what He has promised, not only when we're awake, but when we're asleep as well. The Word of God is working mightily on our behalf day and night. God has a destiny for our lives, and that destiny lies within the promise of the Scriptures. It lies within the Word of God. As we search the Scriptures, we find the life and the destiny that God has for us. God is going to stand by us as long as we stand by His Word because He is committed to seeing His Word fulfilled in our lives.

Innovation

I remember when our son Christopher was much younger, he loved to build things. Even at only six or seven years of age, he would grab a hammer, some nails, and a board and anything that could be built, he would attempt to build. There was a builder in him trying to get out. While he does not work in construction, per se, still today he is innovative in his heart. He is innovative in his approach to worship and in his approach to his recording studio. I believe that no matter our calling in life, there's a builder in us all. There's an innovator inside all of us. God's creativity lives in us and we must learn how to channel that to construct the destiny that God has planned for each and every one of our lives. If we will embrace His creativity, God will stand by His promise until it is fulfilled in our lives.

John Bevere's book *Relentless*, prompted me to dig further into the words of John 1:16. This verse says that from the fullness of Jesus, we have all received grace for grace. One Greek scholar explained that scripture by saying that we have received the richest abundance of grace. In other words, there is no higher impartation than this level of grace. In order for us to be creative and innovate and live lives that are full and rich with God's blessing and favor, we have to rely on that richest abundance of grace that is on the inside of every believer.

But it all starts with believing. So many of God's people fall short of what God intends for them because they can't bring themselves to believe the enormity of power and potential that lies within them. Scripture declares that we have an exceeding abundant potential on the inside of us. Exceeding abundant promises have

An Unconventional Approach

been given to us and we have to release our faith in the grace of God, in the deposit of His grace that He has made inside of us because in doing so, we release God's supernatural ability.

It has been said that the grace of God is the water and the conduit is faith. When there is a break in the flow, we can't blame God. We have to deal with the conduit, which is our faith. We must be sure to keep our faith up, keep our faith activated and our attitude in the right place to keep the flow continuous. If we let our attitude have altitude, then we can surely activate our faith, which releases the power of God's grace in and through our lives.

John Bevere, in an attempt to help us understand what we've been given, gives an example in his book that goes something like this. Suppose you were to approach a freshman architecture student at a university and say, "We now have a new, specific, scientific means by which we can impart to you the full ability of Frank Lloyd Wright." What do you think this young student's response would be? I'm almost certain he would exclaim, "Wow! Sign me up right now!" Once the ability of Wright had been imparted to him, what would this student do? He'd leave school and launch his award-winning career, of course. He would waste no time. Let me give you one more example to drive this point home. Suppose I approach a struggling businessman and say, "We have a new scientific means that can enable us to give you the full entrepreneurial ability of Bill Gates." What do you think the struggling businessman's response would be? He'd cry out, "I want it. Let's do it." And what would that businessman do after receiving Bill Gates' full ability? He'd start designing new products and make business investments that

Innovation

he had never thought of before. Grace hasn't given any of us the full ability of Frank Lloyd Wright or Bill Gates. That would be a grace far too small. No, God's grace has given us the fullness of Jesus Christ. Do you comprehend this? That's ability. That's power. What are we doing with the ability and power that we've been given? Are we like the student or the businessman in the examples, do we run out and put into effect what we've been given?

I want us to again consider 2 Peter 1:3: "By his divine power, God has given us everything we need for living a godly life. We have received all of this by coming to know him, the one who called us to himself by means of his marvelous glory and excellence" (NLT). When we look at this scripture, we see that we have been given everything we need for living a godly life. Everything that we need we have through this divine impartation of grace upon our lives. We have the ability to be led. We have the ability to be creative. We have the ability to be kept from deception. We have the ability to see what others who do not know God cannot see because what we've received is precious. It's not common to man.

Let's continue by looking at 2 Peter 1:4: "And because of his glory and excellence, he has given us great and precious promises. These are the promises that enable you to share his divine nature and escape the world's corruption caused by human desires." Notice the emphasis on excellence. The word "excellence" comes from the root word "excel" which means to go above and beyond. Every Christ follower has the ability to go above and beyond. The reason we have been given this ability is disclosed in this same verse. As we embrace the excellence of God in our lives, we are able to escape the

An Unconventional Approach

world's corruption caused by human desires. The divine nature of God lives in every child of God, enabling us to escape the corruption that would destroy us.

Activate your faith to believe that the divine nature of God indwells you today. Act like a child of God. Act like the nature of God lives in you. Receive the divine creativity of God in you today. We know that God will stand by His promises until they're fulfilled in your life. He will give you the wisdom and knowledge and understanding that you need to see the fulfillment of those promises.

I was doing some research the other day and came across an interesting fact. It seems that the construction methods for building the pyramids in Egypt changed over time. As the designers and workers discovered new and more stable ways of building the structures, they applied what they had learned. The earliest pyramids looked like giant benches and it was a struggle getting materials into place at the highest levels but over time, the designs developed into what we commonly think of today when we think of the Great Pyramid at Giza. The designers applied what they learned to make the structures more stable, grander and easier to construct.

I found it intriguing that even during the building of the pyramids, a more acceptable way to build was discovered and employed. The Egyptians weren't married to their old concepts of building. Even in ancient days, men were willing to shift techniques for a more advantageous outcome. If we are to thrive in life, it is important that we learn to maneuver around the landmines of life,

Innovation

avoid the pitfalls, and make good choices at life's intersections. We need to be prepared to embrace changes that occur in life because that is the key to continued growth. Life is all about about growing.

Our greatest goal must be to continue to grow in Christ. We should continue to grow in knowledge. We should continue to grow in creativity in every possible way to release the full potential of God that is in us. We move in the right direction as we hear God's instructional voice and conceive in our hearts the things that God has promised. We might not succeed at first because it takes time to learn to discern God's voice and adhere to what He is saying but if we will be persistent and consistent in our spirit, with time innovation will be our reality and God's creativity will crescendo in our lives.

Theodore's first art teacher thought his work was too cartoonish, so he dropped out of art class but continued to draw. Twenty-nine publishers said no to publishing his work. But then publisher number thirty recognized his genius and Theodore Seuss Geisel became Dr. Seuss. It took twenty-nine rejections before the door finally opened for Dr. Seuss. Thank goodness he was persistent! You, too, have to persistently continue on. When your spirit of innovation is rejected, you can't give up. God is able to help you shift directions. He is able to help you make the turn so that what is in you can become a reality.

Howard Shultz was laughed at. His simple idea of an Italian espresso bar was rejected by over 217 investors until finally, somebody believed in him and I think we know today that the founder of Starbucks has turned out to have a pretty inventive idea.

An Unconventional Approach

Moses, Elijah and David, whose stories of innovation can be found in Scripture, were all met with a great deal of opposition concerning what God had put in their hearts. Why should we think that we will be the exception as we walk in the innovation that God gives us? We have to couple innovation with determination to see it bear fruit in our lives.

The Apostle Paul prayed in Colossians 1:9, "So we have not stopped praying for you since we first heard about you. We ask God to give you complete knowledge of his will and give you spiritual wisdom and understanding" (NLT). To truly grasp the innovative quality God has put inside each of us, we must come into the complete knowledge of God's will. Many times we grasp maybe ten percent of God's will. Maybe, if we really try, we might understand or perceive fifteen or twenty percent of what God really is saying, what He's doing. But most of us fail to grasp the fullness of His knowledge. I believe Paul wouldn't have prayed that prayer if complete knowledge of God's will and spiritual wisdom and understanding were impossible to attain. God is willing to give you complete knowledge of His will and give you spiritual wisdom and understanding if you will only ask for it and then step out and act. This is basically how you flow in the innovation God sends as you implement the things that God has told you to do. I guarantee you, living this way is out of the box. I guarantee you it is an uncommon and unconventional approach to life.

When Moses and God's people were faced with the Red Sea in front of them and Pharaoh coming up behind them, we see this account in Exodus 14:13-14: "Moses told the people, 'Don't be afraid. Just stand still and watch the Lord rescue you today. The Egyptians you see today will never be seen again. The Lord himself with fight for you. Just stay calm'" (NLT).

Moses came to the people with a word from the Lord. The man or the woman who has the word of the Lord always has the advantage. If you've got a word from God, you've got insight. God has given you complete knowledge of His will for that situation, which puts you at an advantage. There is no doubt that the Israelites wanted to hear from Moses, but I doubt that, "stand still" was what they wanted or expected. The Israelites did not find themselves in a "stand still" kind of moment right then. But God's instruction is often unconventional. God's instruction is uncommon and in order for us to engage it, we have to disengage our brain and empty out our headspace of reason, logic, and human understanding to embrace what the Lord is saying. In short, we must walk in faith.

No doubt the Israelites wanted to run. They wanted to fight. They wanted to hide. They wanted to do anything but stand still, but God wasn't finished speaking yet. Notice His message in verses 15 and 16: "Then the Lord said to Moses, 'Why are you crying out to me? Tell the people to get moving! Pick up your staff and raise your hand over the sea. Divide the water so the Israelites can walk through the middle of the sea on dry ground'" (NLT).

The message was to stand still, until it wasn't. Until the message changed to "Go!" Opportunity awaits the mover. Opportunity awaits the person who will act on the instruction that they have received. Innovation is the result of hearing and then implementing what God has spoken to your heart to do.

An Unconventional Approach

Faith is truly an action. Now, God is obviously not anti-prayer. There is a time to be still, but there's also a time to take it to the next level. After you have prayed, it's time to get moving. James tells us that faith without corresponding action is breathless. It has no strength. It is dead (James 2:26). As the old timers used to say, you have to put feet to your faith. When you hear from God, it's time to quit praying. Get moving. Stretch out your rod.

There was an instruction attached to deliverance for the Israelites. Likewise, there is an instruction attached for your prosperity, for increase to come to your life, for blessing to come to your business, to your home, to your family. There is an instruction attached and if we're able to hear and are willing to obey the instruction, we can activate these blessings in our lives. That's when the power of God starts moving – when we hear and obey. Think of the example of the Israelites. God told them to move and they did. Then as Pharaoh's chariots pursued the children of Israel into the Red Sea, the wheels started coming off the chariots. The Egyptians began to realize that they were up against God. They weren't fighting Moses. They weren't fighting the children of Israel. They were up against God Almighty and He was knocking the wheels off of their attack. Praise God! That's what God will do for you. As you hear His instruction and obey, moving and acting in conjunction with the promise of God, He'll cause the wheels to come off your enemy's chariots!

God is standing with you for the sake of His promise. When God innovates, He elevates. Just as He lifted the children of Israel out of bondage to a brand new level, positioning them for His next

Innovation

word of instruction, He will do the same for you. He positioned the Israelites to advance to the land that was promised to them. God elevated them through the innovative spirit that was given to Moses. God will elevate you through innovation, as well.

Innovation is not a secular term. It doesn't derive from the world that we live in, but from the inspiration of the Almighty who lives in every Christ follower. When God innovates, He elevates, and many of you are about to be elevated in your life, in your business, and in your family.

Chapter Four
Crime Scene

Humor columnist David Grimes once wrote a list of things he'd like to hear but probably never will. Grimes' list inspired me, so at the outset of this chapter, I'd like to share a few of my favorite things I'd like to hear but probably never will. Just once, I'd like to hear from an auto mechanic, "That part is less expensive than I thought," or, "You could get that done more cheaply at the garage down the street." I'd love to take my car in and hear, "No big deal. It was just a loose wire. No charge." I'd love to hear a store clerk say, "The cash registers are down so I'll just add up your purchases with a pencil and paper," or "I'll take a break after I finish waiting on you." I'd love to hear a customer service representative tell me, "We're sorry. We sold you defective merchandise. We'll pick it up at your home and bring you a new one or give you a complete refund, whichever you prefer." I'd love to hear from a contractor, "Whoever worked on this before sure knew what he was doing," or "I think I came in a little high on that estimate." I'd love to hear from a dentist, "I think you're flossing too much," or "I won't ask you any questions until I take the pick out of your mouth." I can keep dreaming that one day I'll hear any of these things but the truth is, I probably never will.

Innovation

There are some words I'd love to hear from God but unlike those instances I listed at the outset of this chapter that will never happen, I can actually read these words right in Scripture. There are a number of injustices that have been committed against Christ's followers. When someone suffers an injustice, they long for justice to be served. The great news is that God has given us this incredible grace, this incredible empowerment that lives inside of us. He has given us an incredible ability to be creative and innovative in our daily lives to overcome adversities and avoid pitfalls, but in truth, we only access a small portion of the potential that God has given us. Well, with these words from God, that's about to change.

In Ecclesiastes 10:5-8 we read, "There is an evil which I have seen under the sun, as an error which proceedeth from the ruler: Folly is set in great dignity and the rich sit in a lowly place. I have seen servants on horses and princes walk as servants upon the earth. He that diggeth a pit shall fall into it and whoso breaketh a hedge, a serpent shall bite him" (KJV).

This passage was penned by one of the wisest men who ever lived, Solomon. He's making an observation that I feel is prophetic as he says, "I have seen foolishness set in great dignity and the rich sit in a low place. I've seen servants or paupers upon royal horses and princes walking as servants upon the earth" (my paraphrase). We've all heard the statement that God doesn't want us to live in the bigger elements of this life. But the truth is that God has destined for each one of His people to prosper, to be successful, to live in the full measure of their gift, to do everything they were wired to do and complete their assignment before the end of their life or before Jesus comes again. I believe this observation by Solomon confirms this.

Think of this quote as having to do with those who are without Christ and those who are with Christ. Solomon says he has seen an evil - those who do evil sit in high places and those who follow God, who honor God with their lives, sit in a low place or walk as servants or paupers upon the earth. Solomon declared that this is a great evil. I say this is a great crime. This is a great injustice. God's people are living below their privileges, below their inheritance, below the wealth of God's grace that He has bestowed upon each one of us. This is a great crime, a great evil upon the earth.

Let us continue on as we consider the words of verse 8: "He that diggeth a pit shall fall into it and whoso breaketh a hedge, a serpent shall bite him" (KJV). We understand that in Scripture, the serpent is Satan. The serpent represents the evil one who puts his venom into your life, his venom of defeat and destruction. But the only way he can get in to inject his venom is if the hedge is broken. I believe that, according to the Word of God, that hedge around the lives of God's people is made strong through our belief and through our confession of faith as we declare what the Word of God says about our lives. As we stand on the promise of God, a hedge is built around our family, around our personal life, around our health, around our business. Everything that concerns us is hedged in by our faith and by our confession of faith and the only way that hedge can be broken is if somehow the enemy can get you to stop speaking the Word of God and get you to stop realizing your potential in Christ.

Innovation

We must understand that there is a reality in the natural, but then there is a more true reality and that is the spiritual reality. Believers have to continue to strive for the spiritual reality and not accept a natural reality that does not reflect the promises of God and the potential of God in our lives. Solomon says that to do anything less - to see God's people living as paupers when they should be reigning as kings – is an evil. You have to be hungry for what God has promised you.

I've coached sports for years, and I've noticed that the hungrier team usually wins. It is not the most educated or the most talented, but those who are the hungriest who usually come out on top. It's time for God's people to get hungry for victory. It's time for you to stop settling for average and start believing for the best, because that is what God has promised you.

I want to bring to light some specific areas where I believe we've committed the sin of mediocrity. Number one, we have made our boundaries too small. So many people make their boundaries too small. They've made God small. They've closed in their life and they've limited their influence. I remember hearing about an old farmer years ago who came in for credit at the general store. The clerk asked the farmer, "Are you fencing in or are you fencing out?" The old farmer replied, "I'm fencing in." At that reply, the store clerk immediately extended credit to him. After the old farmer had left, another attendant asked, "Why did you decide to give him credit just by asking him if he was fencing in or fencing out?" The clerk said, "Because people who are fencing in are always taking on new territory. People who are fencing out are trying only to hold on to what they've got."

If we are going to set boundaries that please God, then we have to have a "fencing in" mindset. We have to be people who have an expansive mentality. In many cases, we have allowed our faith to shrink, allowed our past to shape us. It's not what has happened to you that matters, it is what is happening in you that determines your final outcome.

It is a crime when God's people make their boundaries too small. God has redeemed us by the blood of Jesus Christ. We have been saved and we have been set free, but we understand that the Greek the word for "salvation," which is *sozo*, means so much more. It is a complete term. That term takes into account the body, soul, and spirit. It refers not only to the rebirth of your spirit, but also to the daily preserving of your life. It not only encompasses a spiritual work, but it also includes God's protection over your life, over your family, and it includes material provision for every need you have. Redemption is not complete without divine provision. God wants to crown your life with His provision. It is a blessing to be blessed. It is a blessing to prosper. Poverty is a curse, and Jesus came to remove the curse that we might be blessed through His prosperity. He came to eradicate poverty, starting with the poverty that exists in the human soul because of the sinful nature and expanding to every extremity of our lives.

It's time to reset your boundaries and make God big in your life. Many of God's people have experienced His saving power. They're free on the inside, but they're bound by debt and fear and anxiety and stress on the outside because they haven't experienced God's full provision. God's redemption is not complete without provision, which is why we must reset our boundaries. We should be growing in prosperity. This growth is measurable.

Too many of God's people look back and realize that they are in the same shape financially today as they were ten years ago. We should realize that our God multiplied the loaves and the fish. We understand that He broke the nets of Peter and the other fisherman with an abundant catch of fish when they followed the divine directive of God. Jesus said, "Launch out into the deep," and when the fishermen obeyed, they found themselves in an innovative experience that caused an overflow of blessing in their lives. Jesus blessed them because they honored Him. When we honor the Lord's house, God will honor our house. When we honor God's business, God will honor our business.

The blessings flow out in the deep. As we break the boundaries in our minds and take the limits off God, when we quit believing what our senses are telling us and start believing God, we will see the blessings. Peter's senses were telling him that he and his friends had toiled all night and there was nothing to be had. But Jesus knows where the fish are. Jesus knows where your harvest is. He's better than GPS or any locating device you can have because He is Creator God. The Creator is able to locate what you need to bring you into a great harvest.

It is time for God's people to get a "bigger boat" mentality. I'm telling you, you've dreamed too small. In some ways, you've limited the Lord. It is now time for the enemy to give back to you the things that were taken from you. It is time for you to reap the harvest. You have to declare and believe that it is your due season.

No matter what Satan has done in the past, he cannot prevent you from moving into the future that God has planned for you. You're going to need a bigger boat!

Enlarge your vision. Enlarge your faith and you will enlarge your life. Many times we try to step out ahead of God and enlarge our business or enlarge our lives ourselves. We try to make investments that are not necessarily God inspired or prompted by the Holy Spirit. That's why we fall short, because our heart is not in the right place. But when God is leading us through His incredible Spirit of innovation and creativity, we always have to plan bigger. We will always need a bigger boat because our God is a big God. He wants to bless us - but not so we can waste the blessing on ourselves, having ten cars and ten houses to live in or a big yacht or expensive things. He wants to bless us for a purpose. Once that purpose is in our hearts, aligned with God's will, then there is no stopping you. You are unstoppable when God's will becomes your heart and your passion.

Consider these words from Isaiah 58:12: "And they that shall be of thee shall build the old waste places: thou shalt raise up the foundations of many generations; and thou shalt be called, The repairer of the breach, The restorer of paths to dwell in" (KJV). God is expanding your world. God is causing you to walk down new paths. God is an innovator. He's not subject to time. He moves things by His purpose and by His plan. This passage from Isaiah tells us that when we are walking in God's favor and abundance, we will build the old waste places; we will be influencers upon the earth. We will raise up the foundations of many generations that previously had crumbled because of sin, greed and pride. God is looking for one man, for one woman who will respond to Him. God will use that one person to blaze a trail and restore paths for many.

I remember hearing the story of Chuck Yeager, the first man to break the sound barrier in an airplane. As he was moving through the different stages, working his way up to break the sound barrier, the closer he got, the more the plane began to shake and rattle. The glass on the gauges of the instrument panel began to break as he drew near to the sound barrier and he was very tempted to quit. He was tempted to back off the throttle, but he pressed on, increasing the speed of the airplane. As he finally broke through the sound barrier, everything leveled out. The plane stopped shaking. The instruments stabilized. He experienced first hand the law of breakthrough. The law of breakthrough states that if you can endure, you can achieve a new atmosphere. There's smoother air right beyond this barrier.

So it is with those who wholeheartedly believe God and walk in His innovation. Sometimes you have to endure a pretty bumpy ride, but there's a new atmosphere right beyond this barrier. We are the ones who restore the paths, so we must press on. Restoration is messy. Restoration is costly. Restoration is tiring but on the other side, God wants to use us to create an atmosphere of innovation for people who have not yet learned how to fully release the will of God in their lives.

A prayer is attributed to Sir Francis Drake, a portion of which reads: "Disturb us, Lord, when our dreams have come true because we have dreamed too little, when we arrived safely because we sailed too close to the shore." God is looking for people who are not looking to take the safe or easy route, but who are willing, with God's help, to trailblaze and create paths for others who will come behind them. God is looking for people who are willing to repair the breach, willing to use their faith and speak the Word of God no matter what they feel, hear or see. In speaking the Word of God, they build a hedge of protection around their family, around their children, around the next generation.

Someone has to stand in the gap. Someone has to build the hedge. You can be that person. Don't set your boundaries too small. Enlarge the place of your habitation. Reset your boundaries and call on God to move in your life.

God wants us to touch our world. He wants to free those in slavery. He wants to feed the hungry and empower the uneducated and bless the homeless. God wants us to be world changers.

There is another crime that I want to talk about and that is the crime of robbing God of the opportunity to make our lives rich with His blessing. Every time our faith is limited and we do not obey Him, courageously stepping out in faith to follow the Spirit of truth, we rob God of an opportunity to bless us. The Bible said in Malachi 3:8, "Will a man rob God? Yet you have robbed Me! But you say, 'In what way have we robbed You?' In tithes and offerings" (NKJV). This example from Malachi deals with our giving, but the same premise can apply to any area where we are called to step out by faith. When we push back and don't obey God, we're not hurting God. We're not hurting the church. We are robbing God of an opportunity to bless our lives. As it says in verse 9 of the passage, "You are cursed with a curse, for you have robbed Me, even this whole nation" (NKJV).

Think back to Adam and Eve in the garden. The curse came because they trusted their own reason, logic, and understanding more than the words God had given them. Because of the coming of the curse, they were now doomed to live below their privileges. They found themselves living as paupers when God had intended them to be princes. It's a curse to know your potential but not be able to access that potential. It's a curse to know that no matter what you do, you cannot take the limits off your life. When you hear references to "the curse of the law," that's simply referring to the fact that the law made clear what we were to do. Under the Old Testament Levitical priesthood, the people knew what they were to do to please God. They just didn't have the strength to perform rightly. That's a curse.

Thank God, Christ came to break the curse! How did He break that curse? By bestowing His grace upon us and in us. Glory to God! We have the force within us now. We are no longer cursed. We're empowered. God's grace is now upon us and in us, empowering us to be blessed and prosper. The empowerment that He's given us is His wisdom, His knowledge, and His understanding – it is His Spirit of truth. Let us no longer rob God of the opportunities to bless our lives.

My youngest son Chris and I love to go fishing. One day we were speaking with a very respected fisherman who has been fishing all his life, probably 40 years or more. He shared with us the story of how once his boat got stuck in the mud. In extreme South Texas where we live, some of the waterways can be very shallow. On this occasion, the man had an innovative idea that another boat would come and begin to make circles around his boat and as that boat made circle after circle, it would throw waves of water his direction where he was stuck. At precisely the right time as the other boat was circling, the man fired up his engine, caught one of the waves of water and popped up out of the mud, now able to move to deeper waters.

Innovators always find a way. They never settle for allowing the mud of life to keep them bogged down. Innovators find ways to create the wake that will help them rise above. They are also willing to create the wave for someone else. Innovators bring themselves and others out of shallow living into the deeper waters of God.

Innovation

Chapter Five

Two Trees

I remember a story on a news program about a man in Colorado who was out for a casual round of golf. He saw signs along the path reading, "Dangerous. Don't go off the cart paths. Rattlesnakes in the woods." Well, it seems the man was using one of those new expensive golf balls and had hit it wrong, so it went into the woods. He could not stand to leave that expensive golf ball in the woods so off he went and sure enough, a snake bit him when he was in the woods. Needless to say, that was the end of his golf outing.

The golf course wasn't to blame for the snakebite the man received. There were signs clearly posted telling him not to stray from the path, but the man disregarded the signs and got off path and was bitten. That's exactly what happens in our lives. When we get off the path, we become vulnerable to Satan's attack. Staying on the path means staying in the truth. As long as you are staying in the truth, Satan won't be able to bite you. Circumstances won't be able to stop you. Your mountains won't be bigger than your opportunities. Your adversities will not be greater than the purpose and power of God that is within you.

John 16:13 says the Holy Spirit will lead us into all truth: "When the Spirit of truth comes, he will guide you into all truth.

He will not speak on his own but will tell you what he has heard. He will tell you about the future" (NLT). The world doesn't know the Spirit; it doesn't recognize Him because it isn't looking for Him. You see when you are calling upon God for His creativity on a daily basis, you develop the ability to recognize His voice. One thing we have as Christ followers is discernment in that we are able to recognize the voice of God leading us where we ought to go. We have the ability to distinguish the right path from the wrong path, a good investment from a bad investment, a good relationship from a bad relationship. God has given us a spirit of discernment. Value that. Practice discernment. Remember what you have been given and rejoice. Confess daily that you have a spirit of discernment.

This is such a powerful truth. The Spirit of truth, the very essence of truth lives in us and guides us into truth. You could easily insert the word "reality" for truth. When the Spirit of reality comes at your new birth when you place your faith and trust in Jesus Christ and become a believer, He will guide you into all spiritual realities. Hallelujah!

We have a Guide in this life. Hallelujah! We are not stumbling blindly along. You should be able to outrun your peers and outthink and out-create your peers in any area because the Spirit of truth abides with you. Just as Daniel and his friends who were living in Babylonian captivity had seven times more wisdom, knowledge and understanding than all others because of their position with God, through our new birth in Christ Jesus, we have access to seven times more. The Spirit of truth has come.

Understand that I am not proposing that we have an escapist

mentality. Far from it. So many people want to label men of God who preach faith and victory as escapists. They say we are trying to escape from reality, but that is not the case at all. I am not advocating an escape from reality. I am calling God's people to embrace a higher reality. You see, the Greek word often translated "truth" can also be translated "reality." I am advocating for taking the reality that is in our face each day and forcing it to conform to the Word of God, which has the final word in our lives. The Word of God leads us into avenues that nobody else has even thought about yet. I am saying that we must make the inferior (the world's ideas) subject to the superior (God's wisdom). We must bring natural things under a spiritual order and we do that by embracing the truth of God. What is ultimate truth? Ultimate truth is whatever God is saying.

When we talk about being innovators and cutting edge individuals, at the very tip of the sphere, we're talking about exploring things that the world has never thought about, things the greatest minds in the world haven't yet conceived. The Spirit of truth will guide you into these areas because God is Alpha and Omega. He's already been there, done that, bought the T-shirt. Not only that, but He sees the end from the beginning. He knows what will bring the best results. We should always have the one up and the advantage because truth is on our side.

As God's people, we should not be content with struggling through life because the curse has been removed from us. Praise God! Remember the words of Galatians 3:13-14: "Christ hath redeemed us from the curse of the law, being made a curse for us:

for it is written, Cursed is every one that hangeth on a tree: That the blessing of Abraham might come on the Gentiles through Jesus Christ; that we might receive the promise of the Spirit through faith" (KJV). Those who believe are heirs of God. We have an inheritance. Praise God! And through that inheritance, our ground is no longer cursed. Our lives are no longer limited. We're living in the realm of possibility in Jesus Christ because we believe in Him.

It is a shame when we begin trusting human reason over divine revelation. This is not a new development. It has been going on since the very beginning. Consider these words from Genesis 2:16-17: "And the LORD God commanded the man, saying, Of every tree of the garden thou mayest freely eat: But of the tree of the knowledge of good and evil, thou shalt not eat of it: for in the day that thou eatest thereof thou shalt surely die" (KJV).

Developing a hunger for the right things while at the same time developing a divine dislike for the wrong things will keep you walking in victory in your lifetime. Hunger for the right things determines your outcome. Adam and Eve's desire for a bite of the wrong thing changed humanity's direction forever. One wrong appetite altered the course of human history.

I believe those two trees in the garden – the tree of the knowledge of good and evil and the tree of life - represent something important. The first tree, the tree of the knowledge of good and evil, represents logic, reason and human understanding. The second tree, the tree of life, represents God's wisdom, knowledge and spiritual revelation.

God wants us to feed on the right tree. He wants us to have an appetite for the right things. Every day when we get up, there are two trees in our garden. We can trust and rely on the tree of logic and reason and human understanding or we can embrace God's tree of life, speaking the Word of God, declaring His will for our lives, believing that God is going to cause us to triumph over every situation and overcome every mountain in our life.

We are exercising our faith when we feast at the tree of life. Feasting from this tree leaves us with positive expectation and unlimited ability. But when we partake of the tree of the knowledge of good and evil, we rely on logic, reason, and understanding and we end up limiting God. We limit His ability to influence and touch our lives. Our choice either causes us to live in a big world or a small world. It is all in direct proportion to the size of our faith as revealed by our choice of where to eat.

The Bible tells us Adam and Eve fed at the tree of logic, reason and human understanding. How do we know that? Just consider the terminology Satan used as he spoke to Eve, "Has God indeed said, 'You shall not eat of every tree of the garden'?" (Genesis 3:1, NKJV). That is not what God said at all! Satan was trying to get Eve to question the validity of God's Word and that's what logic, reason, and human understanding does. Human understanding will get you to second-guess yourself. Human understanding will get you to doubt God and His plan for your life. There is always the potential for a "Did God really mean that? Is that what the Lord really said?" to sneak into your mind. Always know that when that voice is present, it is present to try to get you to feed from the wrong tree. Your decision in that instance is critical. If you don't believe how you satisfy your hunger will directly affect your life, consider these words from God in Genesis 3:17: "Since you listened to your wife and ate from the tree whose fruit I commanded you not to eat, the ground is cursed because of you. All your life you will struggle to scratch a living from it" (NLT).

We know that in John 10:10, Christ promised us that we would have life to the full, till it overflows. That's the abundant life of God - full life, overflowing life. When we trust our own logic and wisdom, we will experience the exact opposite. When we trust and rely on human reason over divine revelation, we will always be struggling and scratching to make a living. Our ground will always be cursed. Our fruitfulness will always be limited because we're feeding at the wrong tree. Take the limits off God. Feast at the tree of life, the tree that's infused with the knowledge of God and His Word.

Our God brings everything from the Spirit into the natural. So many focus on their natural situations, wanting their finances to change, their physical condition to change, their weight to change, their spouse to change, their employer to change. But if we operate in the supernatural, if we keep our focus on the kingdom of God, we will understand that God uses things that are unseen to alter the things that are seen. God uses the forces of our faith and the forces of His Word. These forces are intensified through prayer and through the working knowledge of God in our lives. God wants us to have an experiential knowledge of Him, not head knowledge or something we read in a book or heard from a sermon. He wants us to have experiential knowledge of Him so that when we are in negative situations, we will learn to call upon His name. When we find ourselves at impossible crossroads, we will call to Him for direction. Prove the power of God in your life and see that God will use the invisible to change the visible in your life.

People who are depending on their logic, reason and understanding to formulate solutions throw their hands up in despair when confronted with tough situations. You can't search your senses for answers to spiritual problems. What you are facing started in the unseen, and it is going to have to be resolved in the unseen. We have another realm in which we operate. Through the power and direction of God, we are innovators. We can release the creativity of God. The Bible says we have the Spirit of truth inside of us and we operate in God's truth.

We don't search our senses for solutions. The Word of God is the birthplace of all truth, so go to the Word and search the Scriptures to have your soul illuminated and to activate God's creativity. You can't do this by saying a flippant prayer or going to church occasionally. You have to be a voracious reader of Scripture, someone who is hungry for the Word of God because the Word of God stimulates divine creativity. Without the truth at work and living in you, you'll always be limited in the realm of your influence.

Innovation

Chapter Six
God's Justice System

Previously we read a portion of scripture from Malachi 3 concerning the curse. The curse brought about by lack of faith and our disobedience causes us to live below the privileges and blessings that God has prepared for us. The words of Malachi 3 make it clear that when we are not in faith, releasing to God His tithes and our offerings, we are precluding Him from opening the windows of heaven to pour opportunity and blessing over our lives. Through the windows come God's wisdom, knowledge, and understanding - the tree of life manifested in our lives.

God promises us that as we obey Him, He will speed wisdom and knowledge and understanding to us. That is the way He pours out blessings on our lives, through our gaining an understanding of what He wants us to do, where He wants us to go, and how He wants us to invest. God's revelation knowledge is the vehicle that delivers blessing in our lives. What opens the windows of blessing is our obedience, living in such a way that honors God. We have nothing without the Lord, without His hand, without His voice in our lives. We're powerless.

Innovation

In Malachi 3:11, God says these words, "And I will rebuke the devourer for your sakes, and he shall not destroy the fruits of your ground; neither shall your vine cast her fruit before the time in the field, saith the Lord of hosts" (KJV). God wants your business to prosper. God wants your family to prosper. God wants your every endeavor to bear the fruit of His blessing. He will not allow the fruit of your ground to be destroyed by the enemy. God said that as we obey Him and begin to be empowered with His knowledge, He will rebuke the devourer for our sakes. Those things that would have come and taken the creativity, energy, and the life out of our spirit, those things that would try to take the light out of our eye, He will rebuke for our sakes.

Praise God, Malachi 3:11 guarantees that we will have a due season when it says, "…neither shall your vine cast her fruit before the time in the field" (KJV). God, by His grace, will allow things to grow at just the right time. These things will not be birthed prematurely but in season and they will have longevity because of God's blessing upon our life.

Satan wants to constantly devour and destroy what God is building in our lives. We have to learn to rise up and shake that off. I love the story about the old donkey that fell in the well. The farmer decided it was too much effort to pull him out of the well hole, so he just decided he would bury the donkey where he was. He got a couple other farmers to come and they started shoveling dirt on top of the poor donkey. Not knowing what the farmer was trying to do to him, every time dirt fell on the donkey's head, he just shook the dirt off and stomped the ground. The men continued to throw dirt and the donkey continued to shake it off and stomp the ground. Finally, the donkey walked out on level ground because he had learned to shake off the dirt that others were trying to throw on him.

You have to understand that Satan will throw a lot of dirt to try to bury your dreams, your hopes, and your creativity. Every day, you've got to determine to shake that off and stomp the ground, remembering who you are in Christ Jesus. Remember that you are a prince, not a pauper.

Satan is unjust. He wants to make sure that you, as a child of God, do not get the things that are rightfully yours through Jesus Christ. Thankfully, God has given us the wonderful agent of the Holy Spirit whose job it is to bring vengeance upon God's enemies. God will truly fight your battles for you. As Romans 12:19 declares, "Dearly beloved, avenge not yourselves, but rather give place unto wrath: for it is written, Vengeance is mine; I will repay, saith the Lord" (KJV).

What an awesome promise to know that God will take vengeance upon our enemies. That should create a new attitude on the inside of us when we know God is fighting for us. Martin Luther King Jr. said, "Injustice anywhere is a threat to justice everywhere." Don't allow the enemy to threaten what God has already declared is yours in your life. Because God is your avenger, you need no longer suffer abuse. No longer must you be molested by the devil or taken advantage of by the enemy because God is fighting for you. Your faith is an active force working for you.

Innovation

Abraham and Sarah set off on a journey of faith, led by God to become all that He created them to be. Abraham had a promise that he would be the father of nations. The only problem was that he and Sarah were both up in years and up to this time, Sarah had been barren.

In Genesis 20, Abraham and Sarah travel into Gerar and the king of that land, King Abimelech, noticed that Sarah was very beautiful and desirous. Abraham was afraid for his life, so he lied about who Sarah was, saying she was his sister and not his wife. King Abimelech took Sarah to his home but in the night, God spoke to Abimelech: "But God came to Abimelech in a dream by night, and said to him, Behold, thou art but a dead man, for the woman which thou hast taken; for she is a man's wife" (KJV).

Notice that God spoke to Abraham's enemy, and He will speak to your enemies. He will give them a dream in the night. You don't have to worry about filing a lawsuit or getting a high profile lawyer to fight your battles. When God is on your side, God will speak up for you. He will speak out for you. He will silence the mouths of those who speak evil things about you and he will cause your Abimelech to have a dream in the night and be scared to death for his life.

When someone touches someone God has anointed, they are in essence touching what God is doing. I believe with all my heart that if you keep your heart centered on God's purpose, God will not allow man to touch what God is doing in your life. Man will have to take his hands off because God will speak up for you. He will take vengeance on your enemies. That releases you to love your enemies and do good to those who treat you poorly. You can move on in faith, not distracted by thoughts of anger and vengeance. Let God handle it. Let grace handle it. Let the power of the Holy Spirit handle it for you today.

Many of you are about to experience major victory in your life. You're about to encounter a major turning point in your life. Your attitude is about to shift, knowing that God is your helper and the Holy Spirit will take vengeance upon all of God's enemies.

As we move into the innovation of God, we need these types of changes in our mindset. When our brook is dried up, we need new ideas, attitudes and mindsets to create a new stream. There has to be a shift from within because what you've been doing has not been producing the results that you desire. You have to change your habits, which will change your future.

Consider the words of Malachi 3:16: "Then they that feared the Lord spake often one to another: and the Lord hearkened, and heard it, and a book of remembrance was written before him for them that feared the Lord, and that thought upon his name" (KJV). When it says the people feared the Lord, what that means is that they worshipped God. Their hearts turned to God. They stopped blaming God and complaining, "Well, it's vain to serve God. What profit have we seen? What's come out of this? I was better off before I served the Lord." They quit doing those things and instead, feared the Lord. You'll notice that when they did that, the Lord heard them and remembered the praise they were giving Him.

Innovation

Just because you're facing some adversity now, remember you're breaking through. There's a new atmosphere on the other side. Your focus has to move from complaining to worship. When it does, we see from this verse in Malachi that the Lord harkens. He hears it. God heard the declaration of the Israelites and He hears our declaration as well. Scripture tells us that God responds to our declarations of faith. Isn't that amazing?

God had been aware of their complaining before, but He truly inclined His ear - and His power and grace – when the people began declaring His Word as they worshipped Him. The Bible said these people were remembered. A book of remembrance was written before God because they chose to worship instead of complain.

Our worship pulls far more weight than our complaining. Our worship has greater influence than our complaining. Rehearsing the goodness of God and remembering the goodness of God intensifies our life. Focusing on the bad things that have happened and the problems we are facing diminishes us and drains us of our energy. Meditate on God.

We have to remember that God is good and He wants to restore our lives. He wants to repay us for the things the enemy has taken. The longer we hold on to the pain, suffering and mental anguish, the more lost time and opportunity we'll experience. It's time to experience the recompense of God in your life.

When you understand that God is in your corner and the Holy Spirit is fighting for you, you move to a whole other level of trust – you begin to rest in the Lord. If you'll remember the story of the children of Israel when they were hemmed in by the Red Sea on one side and the Egyptians on the other, the Lord called them to the highest level of faith when He told them to be still. Everything in them wanted to do something. Their flesh wanted to take action, to cause something to happen. But the highest expression of faith is rest. When you rest in God knowing that vengeance is the Lord's and that He will repay you for what you have lost, you're about to get free.

Hebrews 10:35 says, "Cast not away therefore your confidence, which hath great recompense of reward" (KJV). If you keep your confidence, you can receive your reward. By possessing your faith, your reward is sure.

Innovation

Chapter Seven

The Government of God

Jesus Christ is the ultimate Innovator and through His Spirit of innovation whom He has put on the inside of us, we are bringing everything under the authority of the government of God. We extend God's government by speaking His Word over every part of our life, knowing that death and life are in the power of our tongue (Proverbs 18:21). The future of our lives is determined by the confession of our mouths.

We are also called to establish God's kingdom on the earth. We are called to run things on earth under the lordship of Jesus. Consider these words from Romans 5:17: "All who receive God's abundant grace and are freely put right with Him will rule in life through Christ" (TEV). But before we can rule, there must be a shift in our understanding. We must come to understand what God said about us and who we really are. We are called to reign as kings and queens in this life through His grace. We rule through Jesus Christ. Under the lordship of Jesus Christ, we are establishing His government. That is the grace that God has extended upon our lives.

Wherever we see evil, we root it out. Wherever the devil establishes a stronghold, we pull down those strongholds. We put on the armor of God, take up the weapons that He's given us, and in the spirit realm, we undo everything Satan is trying to do upon the earth. But before any of that can happen, we have to experience a shift in our understanding.

There is an incredible passage in the book *Relentless* by John Bevere that speaks to this idea. In the book John says, "So let's venture further into what it means to rule in life by the grace of God. We are to go beyond the norm to break out of the status quo. It means we no longer view life as an eight to five job in which we collect a paycheck every other week and then retire, then die, and finally end up in Heaven. What a pathetic outlook on life. That's definitely not how God intends for us to live. We were created for so much more. We become influencers knowing that God has called us to be the head and not the tail, above and not beneath according to Deuteronomy 28:13. Not only are we to rise above adverse circumstances in life, but we're also to outshine those who don't have a covenant with God. We are to be leaders in the midst of an unenlightened world. The Head sets the direction, course and trends. The tail follows. We should be leaders in all aspects of our society, not followers."

So what does this look like in real life? If you're a public school teacher, it may mean that through the gift of grace you constantly come up with fresh, creative, and innovative ways to communicate with your students that none of the other educators in your school system have thought of. You inspire your students in such a way that others marvel. Your fellow educators cannot help but discuss among themselves, "Where is she getting such great ideas?"

The Government of God

If you're in the medical field, then through the gift of grace you may come up with new and more effective ways to treat sickness and disease. Your fellow workers scratch their heads and marvel, "Where is he getting such innovative ideas?"

If you're a designer, through God's gift of grace you put forth the fresh and creative designs that others emulate. You set the prevailing styles and trends that society follows. Your work sells out and you are known as a trendsetter. You're so far ahead of the curve that others in your field are left scratching their heads saying, "Where is she getting such creative ideas?"

If you're in the political arena, through the gift of grace you display wisdom for settling issues that others previously thought impossible to rectify. You lead the way in lawmaking and are elected or promoted rapidly ahead of your contemporaries. Your discretion and ingenuity cause others in your field to scratch their heads and say, "Where does he get all the wisdom and great ideas?"

If you're in law enforcement, by the gift of grace on your life you bring peace to situations in which others have struggled. Just as Jesus knew where to find the donkey, you know where to find the criminals. You pull together the needed evidence to solve the case more quickly than any other detective in your community. Your ability and wisdom are so remarkable that other people in your field scratch their heads and say to one another, "Where does she get such savvy?"

As a businessperson, through God's gift of grace you develop innovative products and sales techniques as well as keen marketing strategies that are ahead of the curve. You perceive what's profitable and what's not. You know when to buy and when to sell, when to get in and when to get out. Other business people scratch their heads, trying to figure out why you're so successful.

When we allow the understanding that we are children of God and therefore, children of exceptionalism to sink into our being, that's when the shift occurs in our lives. Back in the 1950's, there lived a lady who was blind but she loved to go to baseball games. This was back in the day when the great Ted Williams, one of the greatest baseball players of all time who had the greatest hitting average of all time, was still active. This lady said that even though she was blind, she could tell when Ted Williams stood up in the dugout because the entire atmosphere of the stadium changed. When we get the proper mindset concerning who we are in Christ, the whole atmosphere surrounding us will change as well.

When we begin to realize that God is our helper and the Holy Spirit is innovating inside of us, not just for spiritual things, but for every aspect of our day-to-day lives, there will be a shift. The innovation of God will flow through our hearts and out our actions whether we're a designer, politician, doctor, nurse, law enforcement officer, educator, businessman or businesswoman. There's a shift that takes place when you believe that it's possible for the Holy Spirit to help you and reveal to you the very mind, heart, and will of God for your particular career. Nothing can stop you when God is fighting your battles.

The Government of God

Remember the story of Moses and the Israelites at the Red Sea. As they began to move forward under the direction of God, the wheels began to come off of Pharaoh's chariots. God began to fight on behalf of the children of Israel. So it is as we begin to move forward, the Spirit and creativity of God is with us. God will cause the wheels of your enemy's to fall off and God will give you victory. You are unstoppable. There are some weak folks who don't want to hear a strong message. They would rather complain about the system and how the man is mistreating them. But once you understand God's powerful intervention in your life, once you understand that He is fighting your battles, your attitude will totally shift.

I heard that God is the God of the payback. The words of Hebrews 10:30 seem to back that up: "For we know the one who said, 'I will take revenge. I will pay them back.' He also said, 'The Lord will judge his own people'" (NLT). So many times we spend our lives trying to defend our position, trying to defend our stance, trying to defend ourselves against our critics, against those who don't understand the faith that we're standing in. They don't understand the word that God has given us. But we don't need to defend ourselves.

When you understand that God is a God of payback and He will take revenge on all of His enemies, then we can love people. We can forgive people. We don't have to worry about our back. We know God will adjudicate the matter. He will fight our battles. God keeps good records. He will repay. As Isaiah 33:22 says, "For the Lord is our judge, our lawgiver, and our king. He will take care of us and He will save us" (NLT).

I heard the story of a lady who was living up north. She used to let her children go out and play every day but felt it was no longer safe to do so. She went to her pastor and said, "Pastor, there's drug dealers who have moved into our community and they've taken over the street from four in the afternoon to two in the morning. What should I do?" The pastor said, "Well, you need to extend the government of God. Go out and anoint your street with oil. Stand against those drug dealers."

The lady did just that. She went out and anointed her street from one end to the next, praying as she went. The very next day, the drug dealers showed up about four in the afternoon as usual, but around six that evening, for some reason they were startled. They quickly got in their cars and left the area and they never returned. The kids are back playing on the streets again. The streets are safe because this lady took dominion over the situation and advanced the government of God in the earth.

We have to step out in faith and do the things we know God is calling us to do. In 2 Chronicles 20, Jehoshaphat and God's people were surrounded by enemies. Not just one enemy, but multiple nations had come against them. The innovative Spirit of God is always fresh. His mercies are new every morning. His instructions are fresh every day, and this was true for Jehoshaphat and Israel at this time.

Jehoshaphat determined in his heart that he would seek the Lord, and he did. He fasted and prayed and God gave him instruction. In accordance with the innovative instruction of the Lord, Jehoshaphat sent forth the song leaders and worshippers first into battle. Not the skilled warriors, but those skilled in singing praises. As those skilled in praise went forth, the Word of God says that God sent confusion into the camp of the enemy. They began to destroy one another. That's the vengeance of the Lord.

As we trust God, we have to act on His Word and the instruction that He gives. We have to surrender our thoughts, our emotions, and our insecurities to see God move in such a way in our lives. If we do this, we'll find that God will bless us abundantly. Psalm 105:37 says, "The Lord brought his people out of Egypt, loaded with silver and gold; and not one among the tribes of Israel even stumbled" (NLT). God gave Moses an innovative approach to secure the deliverance of Israel from Egypt. Moses obeyed the innovative instruction of God, and God stood as Israel's defense, securing their release and sending them out with great riches. In the same way, God will take vengeance upon your enemies and grant you much favor.

You may recall that after telling Israel they could leave, Pharaoh and his army then chased them down. This is because Pharaoh realized all he had lost with the departure of Israel. You're not a threat to Satan's kingdom without influence. But when God elevates you and gives you influence, you will experience adversity and attack in many areas such as your finances or your family. This is because now, you are a threat to the enemy. You've made a difference through your influence. Don't be deceived into thinking that the attack is a harbinger of failure. Understand that the attack

Innovation

is an indication that the favor of God is upon your life and the enemy doesn't like that. Don't surrender your confession. Don't surrender your declaration. Don't surrender the promise that God has given you.

You are anointed because of your lineage. We are coheirs with Christ, and God will always stand by His children. Those who are led by the Spirit of God are the sons of God (Romans 8:14). We live as the sons of God upon this planet, which is why we can trust God to fight our battles. No matter what the devil throws at you, it can't stick because you are connected to Christ.

James 2:26 says, "Just as the body is dead without breath, so also faith is dead without good works" (NLT). We cannot expect good things to happen if we're not willing to step out in faith. We can't think that just magically because we go to church or because someone said a prayer over us that everything about our lives is going to magically change in a day. We must determine in our heart to take a step of faith. This requires courage and obedience. It requires confidence in God to step out in faith, believing that God's power will back us up.

In Genesis, Abraham was told to go to a land that God would show him. He had no idea where he was going, but had he not taken a step of faith, he would never have seen the fulfillment of all the great promises God spoke over him. The nation of Israel was literally born through him, but that would never have happened had he not taken that step of faith. But because he did, we have an example for all ages of what faith can do.

The Government of God

In Mark 3:2-5, we see the account of Jesus speaking to the man with the withered hand. He told the man, "Stretch forth your hand," and when the man did, his hand was restored. His healing was contingent upon his willingness to stretch out his hand. Had he not done that, his hand would have remained withered.

In Matthew 21:1-7, Jesus spoke to His disciples and gave them instructions concerning where a colt would be tied that would carry Christ through the streets of Jerusalem. In the same way, God gives us the ability to locate the miracles that we need. God gives us the instructions to fulfill natural tasks. As we follow those instructions in faith, doors are opened to divine provision and supernatural manifestation.

Your provision is hidden in a divine instruction. You have to be faithful in the little things, to obey the instruction God has given you in the daily tasks of life. You have to be willing to start at the bottom and work your way up. If you want to see blessing in your life, be faithful in the job that you have. Be thankful for the job that you have and God will give you something else. Be obedient today because God rewards those who take steps of faith.

In Joshua chapter three, Israel was at the Jordan river needing to cross over, but the river was at flood stage. God instructed Joshua that the priests who carried the ark of God were to walk down to the banks of the river and wade in. When their feet touched the waters, the waters began to roll back and yield so that the people of God might cross over. The priests had to get their feet wet before they could experience a miracle of God. The same is true for you; you have to get your feet wet in order to experience a miracle of God.

Innovation

In the book of Esther, we read of a great deliverance for God's people. When Mordecai learned of Haman's plot to kill all the Israelies, he spoke to his niece Esther and said, "Go see the king because there's a great injustice about to be done to God's people - to your people, the nation of Israel." Esther didn't know how she would be received. She understood that she could be killed on the spot for approaching the king without permission. If the king didn't extend the royal scepter, she would be as good as dead but she took a step of faith based on a word of instruction, and favor was extended to her. In the same way, you have to take a step of faith toward your favor.

Consider this portion of the story of Jacob found in Genesis 30:37-39, 43: "And Jacob took him rods of green poplar, and of the hazel and chesnut tree; and pilled white strakes in them, and made the white appear which was in the rods. And he set the rods which he had pilled before the flocks in the gutters in the watering troughs when the flocks came to drink, that they should conceive when they came to drink. And the flocks conceived before the rods, and brought forth cattle ringstraked, speckled, and spotted. And the man increased exceedingly, and had much cattle, and maidservants, and menservants, and camels, and asses" (KJV).

When Jacob's father-in-law agreed to give him all the animals that were spotted and speckled, God gave Jacob an innovative approach to increasing the numbers of those types of animals. Jacob had the word of the Lord in the matter. He set an image before the animals and as they came to the water, as they conceived, they had the spotted and speckled image before them. The image was so powerful, the animals they birthed reflected that image. What made the image so powerful? It reflected the innovation of God.

In our lives, the images set before us will conceive and that's the image we will reproduce in our lives. We must be careful to ensure that the images we set before ourselves are images that God has imprinted upon us. In taking this care, we are stepping out toward the favor of God. We cannot be passive, believing that God will do this on His own. He gives us His innovative instruction, but we must take steps of faith toward our dream and our destiny.

The Bible says Jacob increased exceedingly. Why? Because he had the understanding that God was on his side and God's innovation was working in his favor. God is going to give you ideas to outrun your peers. God is your defense. He will take vengeance on your enemies and He will recompense you. He will repay the things that you've suffered, the things that you've lost. He will repay and give them back.

I heard about a missionary in Mexico who was kidnapped and as he was being held, all of a sudden his kidnappers were startled. They immediately released him and left in their trucks. A few weeks later, one of the kidnappers showed up in the missionary's church. He got saved. As the missionary was visiting with his former captor, he asked, "Why did you let me go so suddenly?" The man said, "We didn't know who the seven foot tall bodyguard was who was standing behind you dressed in white with that giant sword." They had seen the angel of the Lord! God will defend His children. God is the One who takes vengeance upon your enemies.

Innovation

We have angels at our disposal. We have the resources of Heaven available to us. It's time for recompense. It's time to operate in the realm in which God has called us to operate. We are kings and priests and we have an endowment of supernatural grace upon our lives.

Chapter Eight
Digging Ditches

Admiral Joe Fowler was in the United States Navy during both World War I and World War II. He was a naval architect and during World War II, he was in put charge of West Coast ship construction. Among his many notable accomplishments, he is credited with designing two of the largest aircraft carriers of the time - the USS Lexington and the USS Saratoga. He retired from the Navy in 1948 at the age of 54. A short time later, Walt Disney contacted Fowler. Disney had a dream of building an extravagant family theme park in California. He figured that, based on Fowler's success designing large projects in the military, he certainly would have the knowhow to head up the design and construction of the park that he wanted to call Disneyland.

Fowler felt he was up to the challenge and accepted the job. Not only did Fowler head up the design and construction process, but he also managed the park's operations for years after Disneyland opened in 1955. A decade later, Disney had a new dream to build a similar theme park on the other side of the United States in Florida. He wanted to call it Walt Disneyworld and he persuaded his friend,

Innovation

Joe Fowler, to be in charge of the design and construction of that park, too. The Florida project came with even more challenges, not the least of which was creating the park in the midst of thousands of acres of swamp land. By now Fowler was 71. Most people his age were taking it easy, but he said yes again. By the time Walt Disneyworld was finished in 1971, Fowler was 77. Now he could retire.

But when Joe Fowler was 87 years old, his friend Disney asked him to help with the design of his new Epcot theme park next to Walt Disneyworld. Disney had to work harder to persuade Fowler this time. They flew him down to the site and showed him plans for this new mission. Nobody had ever seen such a park before and Disney wanted Fowler to build it. The fire lit up in his eyes and Fowler said yes again.

Around that time, somebody interviewed Fowler and asked, "Why in the world at 87 years of age would you take on such a huge project?" Fowler's reply: "You don't have to die until you want to." He completed the building of the Epcot theme park with time to spare. Fowler finally laid down his drafting board in 1993 at the age of 99. As far as Joe Fowler was concerned, as long as he had a purpose and a mission, he had no limits. He was famous for saying in response to Disney's most outrageous demands, "Can do."

We've already discussed the fact that innovation produces longevity. People like Joe Fowler who start a brand new life in their 50's and don't finish creating until their 90's truly live full lives. They create opportunity for themselves, they never tire of dreaming and are always about having their visions expanded. They are the innovators who do not give up. They make it through and maneuver through the changes of life.

In Second Kings 3, we see a shifting landscape for the nation of Israel. When King Ahab died, the king of Moab rebelled against the new king of Israel. Once again the Moabites, Israel's archenemy, had risen against them. There was a messenger sent by the new king of Israel to ask Jehoshaphat, king of Judah, if he would join Israel in its fight against the Moabites. Jehoshaphat agreed to join Israel in the fight. In verse 8 of this chapter, we see the kings talking about possible invasion routes and strategies. They were looking for innovative ways to fight the battle.

Many leaders fail to plan what invasion route they're going to take. They simply live out of routine, but what has worked in the past will not necessarily work for today's battles. We must ask for innovation. Innovation has direction attached to it. Rather than review what you've done in the past, you should instead be daily asking God, "What is the invasion route?" King Jehoshaphat could have based his battle plan on past experience, past battles won, previous instruction God had given, but he realized this was a new day, a new battle, a new alliance and it would require fresh innovation for the invasion.

As the account continues, we see in verse 9 that they set out to meet the Moabites in battle and initially wandered around for seven days until they ran out of water. At this point King Jehoshaphat declared, "Isn't there a prophet of the Lord that we may seek the Lord's direction?" (verse 11). You see, they had gone as far as they could go on their own. They understood they needed a download of God's wisdom, knowledge, and understanding. Human intellect and reason only take us so far. We must tap the heavenly flow of God's revelation for our lives.

The kings sent out and found the prophet Elisha. Upon hearing their request, Elisha responded to the king of Israel, "If I did not have respect for the presence of Jehoshaphat king of Judah, I would not pay any attention to you" (2 Kings 3:14, NKJV). The king of Israel was granted the benefit of Elisha's service because he came accompanied by the king of Judah. In our own lives, great opportunity often comes to us through our relationships. God uses people in our lives to help us find right paths. Innovators thrive on hearing fresh thoughts and creative ideas. Innovators always sit on the front row. Innovators always take notes. Innovators always receive input. They are teachable and because of that, God continues to expand their minds which produces victory.

Your answer many times is found in the heart of your key relationships. Ruth found an ally in Boaz. David found an ally in Jonathan. Paul found an ally in Barnabas. Moses found an ally in Aaron. The list could go on and on and on. Sometimes the creativity that we need is to be found in the heart of a relationship that we need to start.

So what was the instruction that the kings received from Elisha? He told them in verse 16 to fill the valley full of ditches. In response to the instruction from Elisha, the kings had ditches dug all throughout the valley. When the ditches were dug, the waters came forth and filled all of the ditches. So the people of God had water for the duration of the battle. Their livestock also had water for the duration of the battle. God's will always bring you through from start to finish. He is Alpha and Omega. He is faithful when you follow His voice of instruction.

When innovation meets perspiration, it equals manifestation. There was something these kings had to do - they had to dig some ditches in order to see God move in their situation and defeat their enemies. I remember years ago as we were preparing to build our church in Brownsville, Texas, the land we intended to purchase on which to build the building was covered with rubble. There was rock and rebar piled up on the property that had been left by the demolition crew who had torn down several buildings that previously stood on the property. The grass was grown and the land was unkempt. But in our hearts, we could see God in this land. This property was our provision.

Because the property was so unkempt the price was lowered, which made it very affordable for our church. God caused us to receive this land, and it was a blessing. Very few could see the vision at first because what they saw was so ugly, but we saw a church. We saw gymnasiums. We saw a swimming center. We saw classrooms. We saw cafeterias. We didn't see raw, ugly, undeveloped land. We saw the provision of the Lord. God had prepared a holy ground from the beginning, but we had to take a step. We had to dig some ditches in order to see God intervene.

If you will dig some ditches today, you'll see God's hand tomorrow. Don't be afraid to take a step of faith. Today our property hosts a beautiful campus where hundreds of students attend school and thousands of believers gather to lift up the name of Jesus. Little

Innovation

is much when it's in the hands of the Lord.

God's people had a need and it was their willingness to act on the prophetic word that caused their need to be met. In verse 18 the prophet declared, "This is a simple matter in the sight of the Lord; He will also deliver the Moabites into your hand" (NKJV). You see, their willingness to act would not only result in provision for their physical needs, but it would also lead to the defeat of their enemies once and for all.

Innovators live in the confidence of God. We must learn the language of faith. God calls things that be not as though they were. He deals in past tense. We believe we are dealing with current issues and current dilemmas, but God deals in the past tense. He has already provided all we need. He now helps us maneuver through the opposition as we are committed to speak His Word and declare in the language of faith that this is an easy task for the Lord.

John 8:32 declares, "You will know the truth, and the truth will set you free" (NIV). It's not the truth you hear; it's the truth you *know* that positions you to overcome the obstacles of life. The great philosopher Sophocles said, "Heaven never helps the man who will not act." Faith is action, and that type of faith is required in order for God's dynamic power to move the mountain that's before you.

I heard Dr. Dave Martin say, "Procrastination is the natural assassin of opportunity and the exact opposite of courage." God's people may have wondered at first why they were being called upon to dig the ditches. Why go to all the work? But God was setting them up for victory. If God didn't require you and I to take a step of faith in courage, to step out without first seeing the results, then that would violate His very nature. Remember, without faith it is impossible to please God (Hebrews 11:6).

James 2:26 tells us that faith without works is dead. Faith is a force that moves and changes. Faith requires corresponding action. Faith is activated by your spoken words. Learn the faith language. Eliminate the "I can'ts" and the "don't haves" from your vocabulary. Your most valuable asset is your faith. Protect it., nurture it and grow it.

In Second Kings 4, the Shunnamite woman spoke the language of faith when she told Elisha the prophet that all was well, even though her son had died. She knew that in God's economy, it's always well. No defeat is final in our lives. God told Abraham to speak the language of faith in Genesis 17 when He changed his name to "father of multitudes," though he had yet to father a single child. Abraham spoke the language of faith. In Acts 20, Paul spoke the language of faith. When Paul was preaching long into the night, Eutycus fell out of the window and died. But Paul refused to accept that defeat and instead declared, "Don't be troubled. His life is still in him." Indeed, it was!

You've got to know what ultimate reality is. Are you focused on God's spiritual reality? Or are you living in the limited, lifeless reality of the flesh, void of innovation and the creativity of God?

Jesus, speaking of Lazarus in John 11, said, "Our friend Lazarus has fallen asleep; but I am going there to wake him up." Everyone around Jesus thought He had lost His mind. Everyone around

Innovation

Jesus could have accused Him of having false hope or of being an escapist preacher. Nevertheless Jesus, with grace and dignity, declared that Lazarus was not dead. He said he was just asleep. Jesus was speaking the language of faith.

I want you to declare this is the most prosperous time in your life. Declare that the Creator lives in you, releasing His purpose and plan through you. Abraham, Paul, Jesus, and Elisha would remove the doubters from the room and then declare those things that be not as though they were. It's time for you to ask your doubters to step aside so that faith can be released in your situation. We were created by the spoken word of God. We are forever linked to the spoken word. We are at our best in an atmosphere filled with words of optimism and faith. We are wired from the Creator that way. When you speak the language of faith, you're unstoppable. When you determine to stop renting space in your mind to doubt, worry, fear and unbelief, and instead kick those tenants out, you invite in faith, hope, trust, and purpose.

I heard the story of a man who was making a routine helicopter flight. He often flew from Austin to Dallas, so one day he decided to make the familiar flight without using his GPS. About halfway through his flight, the man looked up and all of a sudden, there was a Black Hawk helicopter right beside him with a digital read out instructing him to tune into a particular frequency on his headset. When he tuned in to that frequency, he was told, "You are in restricted airspace. We are the United States military and we demand that you put your chopper down immediately."

Well, when the man landed and began to speak to the authorities, he found out that he had been flying over former president George W. Bush's ranch. Because he had not been using his GPS, he had mistakenly entered into restricted air space and was immediately grounded. It took him hours and hours of talking before he could get through the red tape to actually be able to leave again for his destination.

That's the way it often works in our life. We are traveling along thinking we're on the right path, but then we find ourselves in the realm of fear. Our faith doesn't work there and the power and the innovation of God will not work in that airspace. You have to be sure you are traveling in the right atmosphere. In the right atmosphere, you can grow consistently as you make the Word of God a priority in your life. Decide that your local church is a priority in your life and that time with God is not optional but necessary. Time in prayer is not optional but required, because if the atmosphere is not right, you will never receive the desired results that you are trusting and believing to receive.

I remember my dad sharing a story with me about praying for a man in the hospital who was in a comatose state. As Dad walked out of the hospital room, the Holy Spirit spoke to him. He had understanding in his heart. This is where the creativity of God comes in. God told him, "Go back in and rebuke the spirit of death off his life." My dad received that instruction and went back into the hospital room and spoke to the spirit of death. Soon after that, the man came out of the coma. I believe because my dad was obedient to speak the Word of God, to follow the creative instruction of God, God was able to bring that individual out of his coma.

Innovation

There are things in your life today that are lifeless. There are things in your world that are not moving. Speak the language of faith. Find the faith atmosphere and remain in it. Your business is not dead, it's just asleep. Your marriage is not dead, it's just asleep. Your ministry is not dead; it's just asleep and it's time for an awakening.

Chapter Nine

Visions and Dreams

It's amazing how four different people can look at the same situation and see something different. I once heard the story of a young lieutenant, his commanding general, a young lady and a grandma who boarded a train together after the war. The young lieutenant was sitting across from a beautiful young lady and her grandma. As they pulled into a tunnel, it was pitch black in the train car. In the darkness, you heard a kiss and then a slap. As the train came through the tunnel, the parties all sat looking at each other with four different thoughts.

The general thought, *I can't believe that young man had the courage to kiss that young lady, but she didn't have to slap me.*

The grandma thought, *Well, I admire the young man's courage, but my granddaughter didn't have to slap him.*

The young lady thought, *I can't believe that young man kissed me, but my grandma didn't have to slap him.*

The young lieutenant's thoughts were totally different. He thought, *What a great day! I got to kiss a beautiful young lady and slap my commanding officer at the same time!*

Innovation

Many people can be looking at the same circumstances but see them in a totally different way. Proverbs 29:18 says, "Where there is no revelation, people cast off restraint" (NIV). The New Living Translation phrases it, "When people do not accept divine guidance, they run wild." The Message Bible renders the verse, "If people can't see what God is doing, they stumble over themselves." Our vision is the hidden force of our destiny. What we see on the inside will eventually be on the outside.

Proverbs 23:7 tells us that as a man thinks in his heart, so is he. Literally every part of our lives line up with our internal perception. It doesn't matter how others see us, it matters how we see ourselves. We must see ourselves as God sees us. As we see in Proverbs 29:18, if we can't see what God is doing in our lives, we will stumble. Our future is based on the strength of our vision.

Frustration comes when what you see on the inside doesn't line up with what is happening on the outside. However, our faith in God anchors us in times of adversity. When adversity arises to threaten your vision, when circumstances are contrary to what you see on the inside, we can press forward knowing that the vision we're carrying on the inside has the ability to not only change our current circumstances, but also to change our future and bring about what we are trusting God for. Determination has to be coupled with vision.

As Anne and I were coming back from a missions trip to Slovakia in 2012, we had a layover in London. This happened to be during the Olympics. We could not get tickets for any of the Olympic events, but there was a triathlon being held and anyone

Visions and Dreams

was welcome to watch along the course. Well, we got there very early so we could get a spot along the bicycle route. There were over 400,000 people crammed into that park that day.

I took a picture of one man who was so desperate to see the athletes, he tied his bicycle to a tree, climbed up on his bicycle and then climbed into the tree. There he was, perched high over the crowd, determined to see one of the incredible athletes from the nations of the world. Imagine if we had similar determination to rise above the crowd using whatever we have - a bicycle, a tree, anything- to gain higher elevation. If we had that determination, there's no limit to what we could experience in our lives. The vision has to be coupled with determination.

Vision is so important. Every believer has the responsibility to discover what God's picture of their life entails and what God wants from them. Each one of us is on a vision journey. The thing about this journey is, it's not so much what happens to you that matters it's what happens *in* you. Don't allow negative things to paint your vision in a different light than what was birthed in your heart through prayer and dedication to God. We need a clear vision and the courage to follow it.

There are four basic things that vision is able to work in our lives. The first thing that vision works in our lives is desire. Vision is always accompanied by strong emotion. The strong passion that accompanies your vision will cause you to never give up. It strengthens your actions, enabling you to do things that are unconventional. Your passion enables you to think outside the box.

Innovation

I remember when Anne and I were dating years ago, she lived on an old country road miles from my house. The road to her house was rough and rocky and her house was a difficult place to get to. My dad used to tell me, "Son, you're going to tear your car up going out there to see that girl." That might've been the case, but you know my passion and desire to see Anne overrode all the negatives that were before me. When you have a vision, you'll have the strong desire and the passion to override your limitations. Don't listen to the critics and the haters. There will always be emotional vampires around seeking to suck the godly desire out of your spirit. These vampires will try to kill your dream, cloud your vision, extract the life from the plan God has put in your heart. Reject these vampires and instead, listen to the still small voice inside you and you will succeed in your pursuit.

We see an incredible story in Acts chapter 10. For some time, Peter believed he was only to reach the Jewish people with the gospel. But then the Lord spoke to him, telling him to expand the boundaries of his concern to include the Gentiles. God did this by giving Peter a fresh vision.

It's interesting to me that we find Peter camped out in Joppa. It was a waterfront city; a place of retreat and relaxation. As Peter prayed on the housetop and meditated, no doubt he had a beautiful view. But God wouldn't let him rest.

So many times in our lives after we experience great victories, we just want to camp by the waterfront and enjoy some downtime. We have no desire to stretch or challenge ourselves with new visions or new dreams. But God wouldn't allow Peter to do that

Visions and Dreams

and I believe God won't allow a true believer to do that either. God knows that growth cannot take place there and He knows that the opposite of growth is either decline or at the very least, mediocrity.

Peter was awakened with vision. God painted a picture before him, making it clear that he was to leave his comfort zone to take the gospel outside of those he was familiar with and go to the Gentiles. Something stirred within Peter - a new desire, a new passion to preach the gospel to a group of people he had never embraced before.

Don't have a waterfront mentality, desiring only relaxation. Realize that God's vision is constantly evolving and stirring in your heart, just as it did in Peter. Thankfully, Peter was obedient to that vision so that today, we Gentiles can also follow Jesus and understand God's purpose and plan for our lives. Somebody was willing to get out of their comfort zone and leave the waterfront. God is calling you to do the same, that you can rise up and expand your boundaries to experience greater things in the kingdom.

When your dream is connected with someone else's dream, that dream has relevance and strength. Think of the story of Joseph found in the book of Genesis. Joseph was delivered from prison to become second in command in the nation of Egypt – second only to Pharaoh – and this deliverance came as he got involved in someone else's dream. Joseph first interpreted a dream for his friend the cupbearer and then for Pharaoh himself. His involvement in others' dreams led to the fulfillment of his own.

So many times people want to go from jobless to multimillionaire overnight, but there's a pathway to achieving that. There are steps that we must take if we are to see the fulfillment of that dream and many of those steps require you to embrace someone else's dream along the way. Can you participate in someone else's dream as wholeheartedly as if it were your own? If you will humble yourself and commit to serving someone else, God will give you a dream of your own and He will give you dream helpers to come alongside of you to help fulfill your dream.

The second thing that vision works in us is initiative. Vision helps us see what can be. It gives us a picture of the future that inspires us to get moving toward that future.

Anne and I have been blessed to travel and minister in the nations of the world. Awhile back, Anne wanted to have a better camera so that she could document the miracles and testimonies that we experience on the foreign field. She bought a nice camera, but then she decided she needed a super telephoto lens. Well, the lens was twice the size of the camera. I like to travel light. I don't bring a lot along with me when I travel - one suitcase packed with a few articles of clothing will last me the entire trip. But now we had another bag to bring along just to carry this camera and its enormous lens. I thought Anne was now working as a reporter for CNN or something like that!

But then I saw the photos my wife was taking with that camera and lens. When I saw what she was able to do with that camera, I conceded and said, "Honey you can bring the camera anywhere, even though it's another bag. I love the results." Sometimes we don't love the process, the work that it takes to bring forth the

Visions and Dreams

vision, but we love the end result. And that's the key to initiative. Vision helps you see what something can become, though it hasn't yet been revealed to your senses. It's much like faith. According to Hebrews 11:1, "Faith is the substance of things hoped for, the evidence of things not seen" (NKJV). Faith takes things that are not clear to you, things that are far from you, and brings them near. Much like my wife's telephoto lens, faith brings it near so you can hold it before you until you actually walk into it and it becomes a reality in your life.

If you don't get up and act on what you see, it's not a vision; it's just a daydream. There are many people who talk of grandeur, who talk of fame and the great things they will accomplish in their lifetime. But it's not those who talk the talk, it's those who walk the walk who accomplish great things. Daydreamers accomplish nothing; it's those who take action on their vision, who take steps toward making it a reality, who make a difference.

If you're looking to own your own business one day, then today you need to get a job and be faithful working for someone else. Think of it as the difference between filling sandbags and building a levy. If you're just filling sandbags, that can be very monotonous. But if a flood is coming, every sandbag you fill is another portion of the levy constructed. You're not just filling a bag, you're keeping the floodwaters back from a city and you're protecting people. You may not enjoy the job you have today working for someone else, but each day that you work hard, hone your skills and serve others, you're working toward the realization of the vision that has been put inside of you. We have to understand that we're not just going

Innovation

through the motions, but we're building a future that God has for us.

I remember several years ago when Anne and I were going through the process of obtaining our master's degrees and then on to a doctorate degree in theology. How difficult it was to study late at night, trying to cram information into our heads in the midst of pastoring a church fulltime, traveling, raising a family, and administrating a Christian school. Had we not seen a career beyond our degrees, we might have given up. That's what vision does for you - it helps you catch a glimpse of the end result so you can continue to press toward it with all your might.

Not too long ago there was a children's movie that came out called *The Lorax*. Anne and I, on one of our flights to London, had the opportunity to watch the movie. At one point in the movie, there's been a great devastation. Someone came in and took out all the forest and all the creatures that lived in that forest fled because there was no longer vegetation for them.

In the midst of the devastation, a young boy stands holding a single seed with a sprout coming out of it, and the boy asks if it is possible that the single seed could restore the whole forest. A voice responds saying, "It's not about what it is; it's about what it can become." This is so true concerning your vision. It may seem small and the task may seem daunting. You may feel overwhelmed, but it's not about what it is, it's about what it can become. You have to focus on where you're going, not where you are.

Visions and Dreams

As the little boy in the movie is standing, he looks down and sees words inscribed on a monument. The words, "Unless, unless" are written there. The boys asks, "What does this 'unless' mean?" The voice again responds, "Unless someone like you does something, nothing will change."

The ball is in our court. Unless someone like you does something, nothing will change. Ask God for a new vision for your family and marriage, a new vision for your business and career, a new vision for your children and their future, a new vision for your ministry and calling. Unless someone like you does something, nothing will change. Vision allows you to initiate the process, to begin to take action with your faith to step into a new beginning and a new season with God.

Innovation

Chapter Ten

Visions and Dreams - Part 2

As visionaries, we are in the know. Visionaries are instilled with desire and that desire brings about initiative to work, so the vision might become reality. The third thing that God weaves into our lives through vision is the ability to prioritize. Vision will prioritize your values. A clear vision has the power to bring what's most important to the forefront of your schedule. When your vision is clear, you are best able to prioritize the way you spend your time. Your day orbits around your vision. Your vision is primary in all of your pursuits.

Vision helps us green light the right things in our lives. Years ago when the Lord raised up Anne and me to pastor LivingWay Family Church in Brownsville, Texas, and develop a multi-campus church and ministry, I had to learn to prioritize my efforts. Before that time, we had been traveling a great deal, speaking in churches and holding revivals. But when God gave me a new vision, I had to restructure my priorities. I had to let certain things go in order to pursue the new vision. The end result was worth the sacrifice because in less than a decade, we saw God raise up a powerful ministry with thousands of square feet of buildings and facilities and a school, all of which instantly made an impact upon this city and region. Had I not adjusted my priorities and given my whole heart for the purpose of pursuing the vision God gave Ann and me, I know the results would have been much different.

The question we have to ask ourselves is, "What vision am I to embrace?" The answer to this question will shape our future. We can't run after every vision. The old Chinese proverb says he who chases two rabbits will lose them both. We must determine to embrace God's vision for our lives. God will give you a singular focus to lead you on the road to your destiny; He will help you prioritize your life to maximize your effectiveness for His kingdom.

Before we discuss the final thing that vision works into our lives, let's recap what we've learned so far. First, vision is the hidden force of human destiny, vision obviously works desire into your life. Second, where there's vision, there's initiative - a desire to set about the work of seeing the vision become reality. Third, where there's vision there's prioritization. Finally, where there is vision, there's innovation. Innovation is the final piece that brings the vision to reality.

The average person may have their own personal dream but as children of God, we are not our own. The Apostle Paul said that we are the temples of the living God, our lives are not our own but instead are hidden in Christ (1 Corinthians 6:19-20, 2 Corinthians 6:16, Colossians 3:3). God lives in us and is in charge of this temple. Therefore, we are called to discover God's dream for our lives. This is not some self-help philosophy or a motivational message to help you become a millionaire. This is about harnessing all of your efforts and combining them with the resources of God to make God's dream for your life a reality.

In Ezekiel 37, we read of a time in Israel's history when they believed in God, but didn't believe God could actually fix their situation. They weren't fully convinced that the vision God had given them could come to pass. Consider these words from Ezekiel 37:1-3: "The LORD took hold of me, and I was carried away by the Spirit of the LORD to a valley filled with bones. He led me around among the old, dry bones that covered the valley floor. They were scattered everywhere across the ground and were completely dried out" (NLT).

Think of these bones as the hurts and defeat people have experienced in their lives - a bad marriage, a bad experience in church, a disappointment in the workplace. These hurts can keep you on the sidelines, but when you have a vision working in your life, it will bring with it a new strategy for seeing it come to pass. It will bring with it innovation. A bend in the road is not the end of the road. We have to determine that God is bigger than our circumstance.

When God unfolds this vision to Ezekiel, he sees brokenness all around him. The valley floor was covered with the bones of former warriors who had fallen in defeat. But God starts the process of innovation in Ezekiel as we see in verse 3: "Then he asked me, 'Son of man, can these bones become living people again?' 'O Sovereign LORD,' I replied, 'you alone know the answer to that'" (NLT).

Innovation

Ezekiel obviously gave the politically correct answer! God asked him a direct question, but He deferred to the Lord for the answer. Many times, God will present us with difficult questions. We have to be willing to look deep inside for an answer as God is beginning to instill his Spirit of innovation in us.

God continues to speak to Ezekiel, giving instruction in verses 4 through 6: "Then he said to me, 'Speak a prophetic message to these bones and say, "Dry bones, listen to the word of the Lord! This is what the Sovereign Lord says: Look! I am going to put breath into you and make you live again! I will put flesh and muscles on you and cover you with skin. I will put breath into you, and you will come to life. Then you will know that I am the Lord"'" (NLT).

I want you to think of this passage as God birthing vision. He starts by confronting your past hurts and past defeats. This process is painful, but know that God is going to give you a strategy that will overcome your past. The innovation He brings is greater than your excuses. After you have confronted your past, He will ask you for answers to the difficult questions to help you discern if you are in this for yourself or for His glory and honor.

Next, we see that Ezekiel takes action. "So I spoke these words, just as he told me. Suddenly as I spoke, there was a rattling noise all across the valley. The bones of each body came together and attached themselves as they had been before. Then as I watched, muscles and flesh formed over the bones. Then skin formed to cover their bodies, but they still had no breath in them" (Ezekiel 37:7-8, NLT).

Visions and Dreams - Part 2

Notice that though the bones came together and were covered with flesh, they were not fully risen. They were attached and upright, but they were not motivated. These bones weren't able to initiate until the vision was fully cast. Every great leader is a great vision caster. Ezekiel had to cast the vision before the bones could take life. He had to inspire the bones to take action.

Innovators are often called to birth a vision in others. To do this, you've got to be willing to stand alone in the graveyard and speak life over dead bodies, over those whose dreams have died, those who have lost their vision. We call these "spiritual flatliners". There is no pulse. There is no energy. There is no passion in them. As ministry leaders, pastors, church planters, you are often called to stand alone in the graveyard and speak the blessings of God and watch as God begins to birth vision and bring something out of nothing. But in order for you to be such an innovator who brings vision to others, you must first have received a vision yourself.

The word "inspired" means in spirit. It's amazing what we can accomplish when we get in the right spirit. When they are in the right spirit, it's amazing what a family can accomplish, what a church can accomplish, what a business can accomplish, what a sports franchise can accomplish. When we are united in spirit, we are unstoppable.

All great innovators were no strangers to inspiration. Eli Whitney was inspired by the idea that there could be a machine that would separate the hard seeds from the cotton fibers. This inspiration kept him up pacing the floor at night. He was inspired to bring change to the cotton industry. As he paced the floor one night, he looked out the upstairs window of his bedroom and saw an animal attacking one of the barnyard chickens, attempting to pull it through the wired fence. Immediately the idea for the cotton gin was born in his heart and the rest is history. It's amazing how when we're inspired, we can see solutions to problems in the simple, ordinary things of life. The difference is we've begun to look through the eyes of innovation.

The story of Eli Whitney shows that one man's inspiration and vision affects life for thousands around him. When we are connected by a common vision, we are an unstoppable army. Just think, if you are part of a sports team, a corporation, a ministry team, or a family, when you're connected to others in your group by a common vision, you are unstoppable.

Consider these words from Ephesians 2:19-22: "You're no longer strangers or outsiders. You belong here, with as much right to the name Christian as anyone. God is building a home. He's using us all—irrespective of how we got here—in what he is building. He used the apostles and prophets for the foundation. Now he's using you, fitting you in brick by brick, stone by stone, with Christ Jesus as the cornerstone that holds all the parts together. We see it taking shape day after day—a holy temple built by God, all of us built into it, a temple in which God is quite at home" (MSG).

God has called all believers to make a contribution. I love the verse that tells us that God is building a home and He's using us all - irrespective of how we got here. Sometimes you may ask yourself how you got to this spot in your life. The truth is, God uses people, circumstances and life events, as well as His Word,

Visions and Dreams - Part 2

to shape us into who we are today so He can use us to build His kingdom. I've watched masons work at building walls and they'll tell you how critical it is that every stone fit in its place. As they are placing the stones, they will break off the rough edges before they put them in place. It's a process. So it is with our lives. We go through a process of shaping so that we can be a part of God's greater plan. We have all been called to make a contribution to God's kingdom. We are all called to impact our world.

In Genesis 4:20-22, we see that Jabal was the first herdsman to live in tents, Jubal was the first musician and Tubal-Cain was the first to work with bronze and iron. There's always a first for everything. Genesis is the original book of firsts. Think about this - before Jabal, where did the herdsmen live? Would they just sleep out under the stars? What if it got cold? God dropped the idea into Jabal's heart to take skins and make a tent. Well, after that idea was birthed, nobody wanted to go back to the old way. Who wanted to sleep under the stars or trust a tree to protect you when you could be under a tent?

Jubal, the first musician, had to forge the first instrument to bring forth beautiful sound. Now music sets the atmosphere for our worship, but there had to be a first musician. Jubal had the desire within him to create a different atmosphere. He found a way to bring the sound within out into the open so all could benefit.

Before Tubal-Cain, there were no instruments for working the ground, for building, or for war. But then God gave Tubal-Cain a vision for how to build these tools out of bronze and iron. He revolutionized the means of construction, harvest and war. He was

Innovation

first in line.

Visionaries create a new atmosphere. Visionaries create new days. That's where innovation comes in. As an innovator, you create a new way for everybody coming behind you. Those who follow will never struggle the same way you struggled to birth what you birthed. God wants you to be an innovator, to be the first to do something that hasn't been done before. God has knowledge of your potential. God knows the measure of greatness that's in you and when you begin to catch a glimpse of His vision, that is a revolutionary day in your walk with God.

The key is to take captive your thoughts. Negative thoughts are a threat to the God vision inside of you. Negative thoughts can disarm you and undermine what God is building in your heart. So protect your ears, protect your eyes, guard your heart. Be careful what relationships you allow yourself to engage in. It's been said that friends are like buttons on an elevator - they can take you up or they can bring you down. Your relationships can compliment the vision of God inside of you or threaten it. Value the vision that has been entrusted to you. You're holding something precious, something God-birthed on the inside.

The vision that God has placed on the inside of you will birth a desire within you. It will spur initiative within your heart to get to work. It will help you prioritize your life, so that the most important things will be first on your list and the vision God gives will help you innovate to bring the vision to pass. Understand the value of what God has given you. If you hold the vision in right estimation, that vision will grow and come to full maturity in your life.

Chapter Eleven
Corporate Vision

I'm reminded of the story of the new teacher at a school. One day the children were playing a game of soccer, and the teacher saw a little girl down at the end of the field all by herself. The teacher thought the little girl had probably been rejected by the other children, so she went down to the end of the field, put her arm around her and said, "Are you okay? Have you been hurt or offended by the other little boys and girls?"

The little girl looked at the teacher with confusion in her eyes and said, "I'm the goalie, teacher. Don't you know anything about soccer?" No doubt that teacher felt a little awkward at that moment.

That's a humorous story, but truly, God has not called us to do life alone. He has called us to live in community and work together. If your vision is just big enough for you, then your vision is too small. A God-vision involves others. Others have to eventually come around you in order for the vision God has given you to come to reality.

Visions thrive in an atmosphere of unity. Conversely, they die in an atmosphere of disunity. Consider the words of Psalm 133:1-3:

Innovation

"How wonderful it is, how pleasant, when brothers live in harmony! For harmony is as precious as the fragrant anointing oil that was poured over Aaron's head and ran down onto his beard and onto the border of his robe. Harmony is as refreshing as the dew on Mount Hermon, on the mountains of Israel. And God has pronounced this eternal blessing on Jerusalem, even life forevermore" (TLB).

There is tremendous value in unity. Wherever there is unity, God commands His favor and blessing. When God commands something, nothing can stand in the way of its accomplishment. Do not misunderstand. Unity does not just mean we don't speak negatively or stir up controversy. When a group is unified, it means the members are all in. They are all involved. They are all promoters of the vision.

I recently read that at most companies, only 17% of the employees are actually considered promoters of the organization. That means that 83% of the people who derive their income from that company are simply wage earners, not promoters. If you want God to bless you, be promoter of the visions He has given to others. Be a promoter of your church's vision or your pastor's vision. Unity means much more than just the absence of trouble makers. Unity is the presence of promoters.

Years ago, I played basketball in high school. One day, a special speaker was coming to our local church and I wanted to be a part of that service. I'll never forget what my coach said when I asked if I could miss practice to attend church. He said I could go, but I might not like the results of my going. Well I thought, *This is church. He ought to let me go.* But after that service when I returned to the team, it was very difficult for me to make it back to the starting lineup because I had communicated to my coach that what I wanted to do was more important than supporting the vision of the team. I know we could argue all day long about the greater importance of church over sport, but the point is that day, I chose another activity over my team. We cannot expect others to make a greater sacrifice than we're willing to make. We have to be an all-in individual or we might find ourselves bumped from the starting lineup.

Great teams execute together. The 1980 U.S. Olympic hockey team that defeated Russia in that stunning final game was a unified team. They did not concern themselves with glorifying the individual names on the backs of the jerseys, but put all of their efforts into glorifying the name on the front of the jersey - the United States of America. We should be united by a common name - the name of Jesus. God has called us to serve to advance the name of His Son.

I remember these words of Ruth, "And Ruth said, Intreat me not to leave thee, or to return from following after thee: for whither thou goest, I will go; and where thou lodgest, I will lodge: thy people shall be my people, and thy God my God" (Ruth 1:16, KJV). Ruth was speaking to her mother -in- law, Naomi. Naomi was an Israelite of the people of God; Ruth was a Moabite, but by this declaration to follow Naomi and serve her God, Ruth positioned herself for great blessing. Instead of just gathering the leftovers from the field, Ruth eventually became the wife of the very wealthy landowner, all because she aligned herself with the people of God. When we are strategically aligned with the people God has ordained for our lives, His blessing will come our way.

Innovation

There is a story about David found in 1 Chronicles 12:16-18: "Other Benjamites and some men from Judah also came to David in his stronghold. David went out to meet them and said to them, 'If you have come to me in peace, to help me, I am ready to have you unite with me. But if you have come to betray me to my enemies when my hands are free from violence, may the God of our fathers see it and judge you.' Then the Spirit came upon Amasai, chief of the Thirty, and he said: 'We are yours, O David! We are with you, O son of Jesse! Success, success to you, and success to those who help you, for your God will help you.' So David received them and made them leaders of his raiding bands" (NIV).

These men had the understanding that God was with David and would give him success. They also understood that anyone who was under David's canopy would experience success as well because of the anointing of grace that was upon him. That's one of the greatest things about unity. Where there is unity, the vision thrives. Where the members are not united, the vision dies. It's so important to understand that when we are in the right place, when we are unified with the leaders God has put in our lives and we help others succeed, we are insuring our personal success as well.

Get involved in God's work and He will get involved with you. The local church is God's plan for humanity. It's not just another activity to fill up our lives. God runs the universe with the church in the center. We should run our lives in the same manner. The church is the center of blessing. It's the center of truth. It's the center of ideas that stimulate growth in your life. We must reach the world with the message that they can belong to the family of

Corporate Vision

God. We must encourage others to come and be a part of God's incredible family. The local church is where vision and innovation are inspired in our lives on a daily and weekly basis. The local church is a place where the lost are reached, people get involved and connect with other believers, and the region and the world are impacted as we reach out and lead others even as we follow the leadership of Christ.

We may give thanks when fifteen percent of the congregation are involved, but fifteen percent involvement doesn't constitute unity. We must have an all-in mentality. The normal wear and tear brought on by the world can pull the greatest team out of alignment; it can destroy the greatest vision. I remember hearing a story about a pastor and a young boy. The young boy was mowing the grass one day and the pastor came by and said, "I'd like to buy that lawn mower from you."

The young boy replied, "Well, it's really not for sale, but I could use a bicycle."

The pastor said, "Well, how about a trade? I'll give you my bicycle for that lawn mower." The little boy agreed and they made the trade.

A few days later, the pastor brought the lawn mower back to the young boy and said, "I can't seem to get this lawn mower started."

The young boy told the pastor, "Well, in order to get this lawn mower to start, you have to say cuss words."

The pastor said, "Oh young man, I'm a pastor and I love God. I don't say those kinds of words."

Innovation

The young boy said, "Well, just keep pulling on that string and it'll all come back to you real soon."

Normal wear and tear can most definitely take a toll on a life. Sometimes we think that we can just keep doing the same thing, that we don't need refreshing or redirection in our life, but that is not correct. We all need refreshing and redirection to keep us in line with the vision God has for us. Otherwise, we will find ourselves out of alignment with His plan.

There are a number of things that cause alignment issues in our lives. The simple passage of time can cause alignment issues. We become so familiar with what we're doing that we lose the passion and the excitement of the vision. We may lose sight of our defining purpose over time. All too often, time doesn't make us better, instead it causes us to be more indifferent and more hardened.

Another thing that will take us out of alignment is what I like to call potholes. We live near the U.S./Mexican border, and sometimes our roads are the last to get help when they've fallen out of repair. We seem to be last in the food chain. Our roads can be extremely bad, especially when they've been beaten by a season of rain, hurricanes and tropical storms. With time, the potholes that form will knock the finest automobile out of alignment.

When a business goes through an economic slump, employees' moods tend to change. People stop working to further the vision of the company. They stop taking risks and are more worried about their personal job security or their 401K than they are the betterment of the company. Any time you find a group of people who are willing to give their all for the sake of the company, you've found a recipe for success. But one pothole of economic instability and the company can trend in a different direction.

You may remember the incredible story of Nehemiah and how God used him in the rebuilding of the walls of Jerusalem. Nehemiah was living in Persia, serving as cupbearer to the king. He had a successful career, but his heart began to break when he heard about the state of Jerusalem. Nehemiah learned that enemies had come and broken down the walls of the city and burned up the gates. The city now lay vulnerable to invaders. Nehemiah could have had the attitude that it was their problem, not his. But Nehemiah developed a heart for rebuilding. He petitioned the king and received permission and supplies to return to Jerusalem and rebuild the walls.

As Nehemiah went through this process, fulfilling what he knew in his heart God wanted him to do, he faced resistance. It's always amazing to me how the enemy usually raises resistance - not when you start, not when you're nearly finished, but somewhere in the middle. The enemy will try to give you an excuse to quit. In Nehemiah's case, he found that the people had begun to sell their fellow Israelites into slavery again.

According to Leviticus chapter 25, it is unlawful for a Jew to make a slave out of another Jew, and yet that was exactly what they had been doing. When Nehemiah first came to Jerusalem from Persia, he used money from his own pocket to free several of the Jewish people from slavery that they might help work on the rebuilding project. Now here they were in the middle of this massive rebuilding project, and the people were acting in disobedience.

Innovation

Nehemiah found himself with a major distraction. Consider this passage from Nehemiah 5:7-13 (NIV):

> "I (Nehemiah) called together a large meeting to deal with them and said: 'As far as possible, we have bought back our fellow Jews who were sold to the Gentiles. Now you are selling your own people, only for them to be sold back to us!' They kept quiet, because they could find nothing to say. So I continued, 'What you are doing is not right. Shouldn't you walk in the fear of our God to avoid the reproach of our Gentile enemies? I and my brothers and my men are also lending the people money and grain. But let us stop charging interest! Give back to them immediately their fields, vineyards, olive groves and houses, and also the interest you are charging them—one percent of the money, grain, new wine and olive oil.'
>
> "'We will give it back,' they said. 'And we will not demand anything more from them. We will do as you say.' Then I summoned the priests and made the nobles and officials take an oath to do what they had promised. I also shook out the folds of my robe and said, 'In this way may God shake out of their house and possessions anyone who does not keep this promise. So may such a person be shaken out and emptied!' At this the whole assembly said, 'Amen,' and praised the Lord. And the people did as they had promised."

Sometimes visionaries have to take drastic steps to refocus

the team, so that the vision might come back into view. Over time people get familiar; their passion, drive and desire can wane. Potholes come in our path. We face negative circumstances, we lose personnel, our resources are diminished and so we begin to compromise the vision, to modify it. Nehemiah refused to do this. He refused to let the Israelites be a reproach among the heathen nations by allowing the pagans to see them acting that way. Nehemiah would not allow the nations that surrounded them to see their lack of unity.

Nehemiah had to call a time out, as every great leader has to from time to time. He had to realign his team's vision. He had to react to what he was witnessing in his team. Nehemiah realized that if God's people did not get back into obedience, God could not bless them. This was no time for them to forsake God's blessing! They needed God's favor and blessing if they were to complete the rebuilding of the walls and see God's city restored in that region. Nehemiah had to have a determined spirit. No matter how much he wanted to continue to work, he knew that he had to stop and invest in the vision.

As leaders, we have to be innovative in the ways we connect the peoples' hearts and minds with the vision. This is so important because if a disconnect occurs, the wheels will begin to come off the process and the vision will never be fulfilled. Dewitt Wallace had a vision for a pocket-sized publication full of inspirational stories. He went to several different publishers pitching the idea and was rejected time after time. Finally, he decided to self-publish the work and started distributing a few copies among his friends.

Innovation

The publication was well received, to say the least. Today, over 17 million readers subscribe to *Reader's Digest*. Dewitt connected the hearts of others to his vision, and now millions buy into it.

As we have expanded our church to include multiple campuses in different cities, we cannot physically be at every service in every location. We use technology to stream the message to the different campuses. With this format, it could be very easy for people to stray from the vision. What we refer to as "vision drift" can occur quickly if we're not diligent. The key to preventing vision drift is to faithfully communicate the vision using innovative means. Habakkuk 2:2 tells us to write down the vision and make it plain so that others can run with it. Communication of the vision has to be clear and it has to occur frequently in order to keep your team on track.

When the vision is made plain and there is unity among the team, the work of God thrives. Failure to make the vision plain will result in a lack of unity as each member pursues his own vision or his own interpretation of the corporate vision. Two visions equal division. One God-inspired vision pursued corporately by believers can change the world.

Chapter Twelve
To My Haters and Underestimators

Every visionary will eventually have to deal with those set on destroying the dream. Conceiving the dream is one thing; fulfilling the dream is something else entirely. We understand that we must discover God's vision for our lives. It's much easier to steward God's vision for our lives than defend our own vision. We know that when we are pursuing God's vision, God is on our side and He fights our battles. No weapon formed against us can prosper, but we will face opposition. As Andy Stanley says, "If you've ever shared a vision, you're fully aware of four things: Number one, visions are easy to criticize. Number two, visions attract criticism. Number three, visions are difficult to defend. Number four, visions often die at the hands of critics."

From the time that we enter into this world, we are faced with criticism. All of us have gone to the hospital before to see a newborn child. As you look through the little window at all the precious babies in the nursery, you can hear a myriad of comments about how big the ears are, how big the head is, how big the nose is, how little hair the child has, how much hair the child has. From our earliest moments on earth, we are faced with scrutiny. We must own the fact that criticism is a way of life.

Innovation

Holding on to a dream under the pressure of criticism is difficult. If we wait for the approval of others to gavel into existence the dream that God has placed in our hearts, many of us will never even get started on the journey to bringing that dream to reality. Perhaps you've heard the story of the three men who were each carrying two sacks. A passerby asked the first man, "What is in the sacks?"

"The sack on my back is filled with all the good things that have happened to me," the first man said. "The sack on the front is filled with all the bad." The man was constantly faced with the bad things so he couldn't even see the good on his back.

The stranger asked the second man the same question, but received the opposite response. "The sack on my back is filled with the bad things that have happened to me," he said, "and the sack on the front is filled with the good things." At least the second man could see the good and was not focused on the negative. But both of the sacks being so full weighed the man down and made life a burden.

Finally, the stranger asked the third man the same question. "The sack on my chest is filled with my accomplishments and victories," he said. "The sack on my back is empty."

"Why is it empty?" the stranger asked.

"I put all my mistakes, failures, guilt, shame and criticism in that sack, and I cut a hole in the bottom to release them. That way, I'm weighted in the front more than the back, so I keep moving forward. In fact, the empty sack in the back acts like a sail, catching the wind to move me ahead."

To My Haters and Underestimators

We should be like the third man, always moving forward, without being weighed down with the negativity and criticism of others, but fully alive in the vision God has given us. As an innovator who is wired for creativity, we can't afford to be weighed down by yesterday's failures or the unbelief of those who can't see what God has placed in our heart.

There are many examples in Scripture of those who overcame adversity and pushed past their critics to fulfill the vision God placed in their heart. In the previous chapter, we discussed the example of Nehemiah. God gave him a vision to rebuild the walls of Jerusalem and though Nehemiah met great adversity from outside sources and even from those aligned with him, he persevered to see the work completed and the vision become a reality. God gave Joseph a vision that one day, his brothers and parents would bow before him. Though Joseph was sold into slavery by his brothers and was wrongly imprisoned in Egypt, he pushed through the adversity to see the vision come to pass. There are so many more examples we could cite of those who serve as living examples of what can happen when a person is willing to persevere to see God's vision for their life come to pass.

When an idea is first birthed in our heart, it's fresh and new. The new vision has a romantic appeal to it. We relish the idea of change and pursuing something new, but as we settle into the vision, we begin to understand that not everyone will buy into it. Not everyone will support it. Some people tend to give up and shut down when their dream is confronted with resistance. Others are fueled by opposition. They don't allow their haters to pollute or dilute what they're carrying in their hearts.

Innovation

I heard of a talented high school quarterback who was projected to go on and do very well in college. He was setting records at his local high school, but then one reporter from a local newspaper took exception to the young man and began to write critical articles. This reporter criticized the way the young man threw the ball and declared that he wasn't fast enough and didn't have the height to play at the next level. The young man began to focus on the criticisms of that one reporter and it diminished his game. He never did play after high school because he allowed himself to focus on what one man was saying. If all you focus on is the negative comments of your critics, it will diminish your creativity and even the ability that God has given you.

Returning to the story of Nehemiah, one of his greatest critics was a man named Sanballat. Sanballat was the governor of Samaria. He had much to lose should the walls of Jerusalem be rebuilt. Up to this time, the enemies of the Jews could come and go in the city as they pleased. They could continue to threaten the Jews as the residents of Jerusalem had no protection, but if the walls were rebuilt, Sanballat and others like him would lose the control they currently exercised over the Jews. So Sanballat began to criticize the rebuilding efforts. Consider his words, found in Nehemiah 4:1-2: "But when Sanballat heard that we were building the wall, he was angry and in a great rage, and he ridiculed the Jews. And he said before his brethren and the army of Samaria, What are these feeble Jews doing? Will they restore things [at will and by themselves]? Will they [try to bribe their God] with sacrifices? Will they finish up in a day? Will they revive the stones out of the heaps of rubbish, seeing they are burned?" (AMP).

To My Haters and Underestimators

Just like happened with Nehemiah, as you begin to pursue the vision God has given you, critics will begin to attack to try to convince you that you are inferior or not up to the task at hand. Sanballat was bringing up past failures to diminish the confidence of the Jews. He reminded them of their inadequacies over the previous 100 years and of their lack of strength. He questioned if suddenly now their God and their law would somehow rebuild the walls. Would they complete the work in a day? How would they revive the charred stones from the heaps of the rubbish? Our enemies will attempt to mire us down in the minor details. We must never focus on those things that are of micro-importance where our vision is concerned.

There are two things that bring negative reactions to a vision – change and holes in the plan. Change plays into the insecurity of others. Critics will focus on known facts and history but visionaries change history. Legend has it that when Robert Fulton, the designer of the first practical steam engine, was preparing to start the engine for the first time, there were critics lined up along the riverbank saying that engine would never start. Well, when the engine came to life and began shooting out steam and the boat began to move down the river, the critics changed their chant to, "It'll never stop!" The point is, you'll never escape critics. They will use known facts and past history to dispute you to the end.

While it is true that many visions are birthed from the fertile soil of history, many times history is also used to bury the vision. Focusing on past experiences as well as the failures of others can kill the vision. Change – stepping out into new frontiers - brings the insecurities of others to the surface. You have to stay focused on what God has told you and realize that change is not readily welcomed. The ironic thing is that change is actually the only thing we can count on.

Many years ago when the Lord gave us the vision to come to Brownsville, we were in desperate need of land on which to build our first church. The building we had been renting was about to be condemned by the city and torn down. We had just months to make other arrangements for a meeting space. It was obvious we could not remain meeting where we were and yet, many of the folks in our small church were resistant to change. They could not see that God was doing a new thing.

God moved miraculously in a span of a couple weeks, as He brought in enough money for us to purchase land and prepare to build. I told the story earlier in this book of the condition of the land when we first looked at it, but God transformed that piece of property into the beautiful space that we occupy today. God had earmarked the property for this purpose hundreds of years before we ever showed up on the scene. Though the change was not welcomed by all, though the task seemed daunting in the natural, in the spiritual, God had already made provision for us. Visionaries have to have faith that God has prepared in advance for you. Though you can't always see those preparations, you have to take steps of faith in order to see the vision come to pass.

A second reason we face criticism is there may be perceived holes in the vision. If people can't trace a clear path from A to Z in the ultimate fulfillment of the vision, we will hear criticism. When

To My Haters and Underestimators

we step out in faith, there will always be questions concerning of how things will come to pass. Every innovator faces the criticism. You may see the full picture, but others can't see it. It's important for an innovator to step into other peoples' shoes if they are to override the criticism.

There once was a lady who was waiting in the airport terminal for her flight to board. Before sitting down to wait, she bought some cookies and stuck them in her purse. Seated next to her in the terminal was a well-dressed businessman. As they waited, the man reached down and took a cookie. The lady couldn't believe that the man had helped himself to one of her cookies! In response, she reached down authoritatively and took a cookie for herself. This continued with each one taking a cookie until they came to the last cookie in the package, which the man offered to the lady with a smile. It took everything within the lady not to lash out against the gentleman who had so rudely eaten half her cookies!

Finally, the call came for the lady's flight to board. When she was seated on the airplane, she reached into her purse and there was her unopened box of cookies. She had been eating from the gentleman's box of cookies the entire time! The lesson we can take from this: It's easy to be critical when we don't see the big picture.

There once was a couple who moved into a new neighborhood. One morning while the couple was eating breakfast, the wife looked out the window and saw her neighbor hanging wash on the line to dry. She noticed the wash was dingy and dirty. She said to her husband, "That neighbor lady doesn't know how to wash. Her clothes aren't clean. I wonder if she's even using any detergent."

Innovation

Day after day went by and the wife made the same comment: "I can't believe the neighbor doesn't know how to wash. I can't believe they actually wear those dingy looking clothes." A few weeks later the woman looked out the window and the clothes were as clean and bright as could be. She was so surprised. She called her husband in and said, "Look, honey. Our neighbor finally learned how to wash. I wonder what happened."

The husband smiled and said, "Honey, I got up early this morning and cleaned our window." You see, many times this issue isn't someone else's performance, it's our perception that makes the difference. Never judge a work in progress. Just because you perceive holes in the vision does not mean they are really there; the work is in progress. Great works take years to develop.

Chapter Thirteen
A Work In Progress

I recently heard of a memorial to Crazy Horse, the famous Lakota native american warrior, that is being built in the Black Hills of South Dakota. In 1948, Korczak Ziolkowski was commissioned by Lakota Chief Henry Standing Bear to design a mountain carving to honor the famous Lakota leader. The great irony is that Crazy Horse resisted being photographed when he was alive. I wonder what he would have thought about his image being carved into a 563-foot- high statue on the face of the Black Hills!

Ziolkowski invested more than 30 years of his life to carving this monument that is intended to be eight feet higher than the Washington Monument and nine times larger than the faces on Mount Rushmore. Following his death in 1982, Ziolkowski's family has carried on the vision their father birthed. The projected completion date is 2050. With the project taking so long to complete, it begs the question, why spend a lifetime carving one larger-than-life statue? Ziolkowski's answer, "When your life is over, the world will ask you only one question - did you do what you were supposed to do?"

Great works take time to develop, so we should never judge a

Innovation

work before its time. When last we saw Nehemiah, he was coming under scrutiny for the vision that God had given him. Sanballat, the governor of Samaria, was openly critical of Nehemiah's efforts. He had mounted an attack against Nehemiah and the group of laborers working alongside him. But Nehemiah and the people had a mind to work (Nehemiah 4:6). They kept their focus. They kept moving forward in spite of the enemy's resistance.

The story continues in Nehemiah 4:7-8: "But when Sanballat, Tobiah, the Arabians, Ammonites, and Ashdodites heard that the walls of Jerusalem were going up and that the breaches were being closed, they were very angry. And they all plotted together to come and fight against Jerusalem, to injure and cause confusion and failure in it" (AMP).

As the vision grows stronger, the enemy begins to lose ground. Enemies don't like to lose ground, so they will always ramp up their efforts to stop what God is building. Sanballat gathered the surrounding cities against the Israelites. Soon, word began to spread about the impending war. Other Jews began to encourage the builders to leave their posts, saying that their lives were in danger. Some of the workers began to walk off the job. It's amazing how quickly some of those who have a mind to work can give up. As the criticism grows, we lose our determined spirit. It affects our overall attitude towards the vision. The Israelites were finding there was more rubbish to sift through than they initially thought, the project was larger than they anticipated, they were tired, the thrill was gone, and now there were a multitude of voices calling on them to quit. All of these things amplified the negatives and their peace began to bleed.

A Work in Progress

Many people who come to Christ soon suffer the "new believer's blues." We've all suffered criticism, but many new believers in Christ are not ready for the criticism that comes from family who do not follow Christ, who have not yet seen what they've seen. As criticism mounts, they are reminded of what they – and others - are not. They want others to celebrate their newfound love for Christ when in reality, many despise them for their joy and the peace that they now have in their heart. This leads to the new believer's blues, which shakes their newfound contentment in Christ. It discourages those who may have wanted to step out in faith to the point that they no longer strive to do so. They are no longer interested in expanding their lives or careers. They do not seek growth that they might be a blessing to generations to come. They no longer seek to finance missions and the outreach of the local church.

You have to press through this season of resistance and realize you are now an agent of change that God will use to bring others from spiritual darkness to spiritual light.

What at first meets resistance, many times will eventually be accepted through persistence and repetition. Don't accept rejection as a sign of failure; view it as a necessary reality on the way to the fulfillment of the vision that God has placed in your heart.

You must not allow your vision to die at the hands of the dream destroyers. Stephanie wants to date a Christian guy. She believes that God will give her a spouse who is a believer and a God-fearing man. But those around her insist there are no Christian guys available. They tell her it's impossible to find a good man anymore. Stephanie has to continue to believe and remain true to her convictions, not giving in to those naysayers who criticize because of bad experiences they might have had. Stephanie cannot allow the dream destroyers to kill her God-given vision.

Ben wants his daughter to serve Christ and love Jesus all her days. Those around Ben tell him that kids are going to go into the world for a while. They have to taste of the world and sin, and then maybe they will come back to Christ in their later years. As a dad, Ben has to stay committed to the vision God has given him that his daughter can serve God and will serve God, regardless of what others are saying.

Tom and Sue have a vision to be debt free. They have a vision to be strong financially, but others are saying that in today's economy, that's an impossibility. They tell them to accept the fact that they'll be in debt all of their lives. They tell them to accept the fact that they have to have credit cards to make it today. Tom and Sue have to stay committed to their God-given vision to live debt free, regardless of what those around them who've failed might say.

Your vision will outlast your critics if you hold true to it. Nehemiah 6:15-16 records the details of Nehemiah's victory: "So the wall was finished on the twenty-fifth day of the month Elul, in fifty-two days. When all our enemies heard of it, all the nations around us feared and fell far in their own esteem, for they saw that this work was done by our God" (AMP).

It is so important to focus beyond your struggle. Great athletes - from marathon runners to long distance swimmers to triathletes - understand the power of focusing beyond the pain and the struggle. I read an article that told of how marathon runners speak to themselves, telling their bodies that they have more energy left. They tell themselves, "You can do this. You will finish strong. You will make it to the finish line. Don't let up. Stay with it. You have what it takes." They get a vision of the finish.

We understand that in the process, Nehemiah had to keep the people focused. Even when there was a threat of destruction and of loss of life, during verbal criticism, the people had to remain focused. You see, your purpose has to be bigger than your distraction.

Notice that in verse 16 it says when the enemy saw that the walls were rebuilt, they perceived that the work was done by God. They knew that what had been accomplished was impossible in the natural. Thankfully, we serve a God who masters impossible situations. We serve a God who is innovative. He is creative in every way.

We have to learn to show our enemies the door and evict critical thoughts from our mind. We have to learn how to shake off criticism and take another step toward the realization of our vision. Don't rent space in your mind to thoughts of defeat. Instead, cripple your enemies by allowing them to see that God is with you as you continue on against insurmountable odds to see the fulfillment of what you believe for.

The more your critics work to bury you, the more insistently you must shake off their attacks. Develop a resilient spirit. Don't be distracted by others' battles. Choose your own battles and choose them wisely. The lady who cleans our house called the church one day, frantic because there was a snake inside the mop bucket in the garage. I had to choose whether I would stop what I was doing for the Lord at that moment and leave to deal with the snake in the bucket, or if I would deal with it later. I chose to finish what I was doing, and then I went to deal with the snake in the bucket. When I arrived home, I saw it was just a small snake that had crawled up in the bucket, but from the reaction of our housekeeper, you would have thought it was a mighty python! The point I'm trying to make is you must not go chasing after other peoples' snakes. That will result in setbacks to fulfillment of the dreams God has given you.

Chapter Fourteen
Responding to Critics

It's been said that it's not what happens to you that matters, but how you respond that makes the difference. We will all face criticism and we must all fight the urge to be critical. Some people are critical by nature. A critical spirit is infectious. It's like a cancer. It moves into your soul and eats away at your attitude, your perception, and the way you treat others. A man who had an accident asked the driver of the other car, "Why don't you learn how to drive? You're the fourth person who hit me today!" A woman whose husband just spent $4,000 on laser eye surgery said, "Even after spending all that money, you still don't see things from my point of view!" From some people's perspectives, what you do will never be good enough. It's always the other person's fault; they'll never measure up.

In his book on vision, Andy Stanley says that there are three ways to respond to our critics. The first way to respond is in prayer. Consider Nehemiah's example seen in Nehemiah 4:4-5: "Hear us, our God, for we are despised. Turn their insults back on their own heads. Give them over as plunder in a land of captivity. Do not cover up their guilt or blot out their sins from your sight, for they have thrown insults in the face of the builders" (NIV).

Because Nehemiah's initial response was to cry out to God in prayer, he didn't allow his enemies to become the focus of his attention. If we focus on the accusations of our critics, we play into their game. If we bottle up our emotion, it leads to depression. If we dump our angst on innocent bystanders, it complicates things. If we pour our disappointment and anxiety out to the Lord, He provides the strength to overcome. This is reason enough to stay vision-centered, not critic-centered.

David cried out to God when he was faced with enemies on all sides – and he didn't sugarcoat things. Consider his words found in Psalm 5:9-10: "For there is no faithfulness in their mouth; their inward part is exceeding wickedness. Their throat is an open sepulcher; they flatter with their tongue. Destroy Thou them, O God! Let them fall by their own counsels. Cast them out in the multitude of their transgressions, for they have rebelled against Thee" (NKJV).

It is an expression of trust to take our deepest hurts to the Lord. How important it is to manage our emotions and stay encouraged no matter what we're going through. Nehemiah understood he was pursuing God's vision. His responsibility was to keep himself built up in that vision, so he turned to God in prayer when he was tempted to get discouraged. Many would have lashed out in the flesh, but Nehemiah got on his knees and trusted God. He turned to God, who was able to take vengeance upon his enemies. God is in control of seeing that His vision comes to fuitiion.

When David was discouraged because Saul was chasing him down, trying to kill him, he sought the Lord. He told God what he was feeling, pouring out his emotion to God so that he could stay vision-centered. Even when David thought he had lost all at Ziglag, the Bible said he encouraged himself in the Lord. He turned to the Lord and found the courage to continue to press forward.

Take courage in the Lord today. Find your strength in the Lord. He has given you the power to overcome because He gave you the vision in the first place. He knew you were the one to run with the ball. He called you to be a difference maker. Don't doubt the vision in the face of criticism. Stay encouraged.

When we pray in the face of scrutiny, criticism is put in its proper context. It's not up to us to defend ourselves or respond to our critics. It's up to us to pray and allow God to deal with them. When criticism is held up against God's infinite resources – not against our limited ability - it loses its power. When we're able to release our frustration with criticism to the Lord, it allows our creativity and innovation to continue to flow.

A young man wrote a college paper for his economics class on his vision for overnight mail delivery. The professor took a red pen and gave him a "C" for his efforts, writing at the top of the page, "Do not dream of things that cannot happen." The young man left school and started Federal Express. I wonder where that professor is today. You and I have the ability to override our critics by simply praying and releasing our frustration to God so that His dream can continue to live in us.

In over 30 years of ministry, I've had many opportunities to be discouraged, to throw in the towel. I'm so glad that despite those opportunities, I stayed determined in spirit. My wife and I determined in our hearts to overcome, no matter what came against us. Every time the enemy sends discouragement into your life, you have to remember he is only trying to stop something that God has ordained for you to do. You're a threat to the enemy's kingdom or he wouldn't be fighting you.

Joel Osteen talked about the positive effects of encouragement. He said even Henry Ford benefited from encouragement in his early days. One of Ford's boosters was none other than Thomas Edison. Ford was introduced to Edison as "the man trying to build a car that runs on gasoline." When Edison heard this, his face lit up. He slammed his fist on the table and said, "You've got it! A car that has its own power plant - that's a brilliant idea." Up to that point, Henry Ford had dealt with many naysayers. He had just about determined that he would give up. But then along came Edison who spoke faith into him. That was a turning point in Henry Ford's life. Ford thought he had a good idea, but then he started to doubt himself. Then along came one of the greatest minds who ever lived and gave Ford his complete approval. A simple vote of confidence helped launch the automotive industry.

We don't realize the power we hold. We don't always realize what it means when we tell somebody we believe in them.

Another way we can respond to our critics is to remember what the Lord has already done. Nehemiah 4:14 says, "And I looked, and rose up, and said unto the nobles, and to the rulers, and to the rest of the people, Be not ye afraid of them: remember the Lord, which is great and terrible, and fight for your brethren, your sons, and your daughters, your wives, and your houses" (KJV).

Nehemiah stopped to remember who it was that brought him to Jerusalem. The word "remember" grabs our attention. The prefix "re" is an attaching word. It's a word that references doing something again. "Member" means to be attached to a thing. Therefore, when we see the word "remember" as used by Nehemiah, we can understand it to mean to rejoin oneself with the reality of the vision that God gave you. Persecution will arise but as we remember all that God has done, we see there is a purpose that is greater than any resistance we encounter. It is important to keep our faith alive and our voice of victory and confession strong, even in the midst of great persecution.

We have to believe in the power of the vision. It is greater than any negative tongue that may rise against you. Think of the vision as a seed. We know that a seed must go in the ground and die or it abides alone. Seeds represent cycles and new beginnings. Think of the cycle of wheat. Every kernel is first born in the head of wheat, then the wheat is cut down. Once the wheat is cut, it is bundled together, thrown onto a wagon and taken to the threshing room floor where the chaff is separated from the wheat kernel. The kernels are then put aside to wait for the day when they are planted in the earth to repeat the cycle again. The full process of a seed always involves some sort of adversity or persecution, but there is always a promise of harvest at the end. What can we learn from the lesson of the seed? Persecution makes us stronger. Testing reveals the strength of the seed that God has placed in our hearts.

Innovation

Nehemiah had this time of remembrance not only to remember who it was that brought him to Jerusalem, but also to allow himself to be reconnected in his heart with the vision that had first captured his attention way back in Persia. In doing this, he was preparing himself anew to be a vision caster, to help others rise above the critics to pursue the vision God had given.

Nehemiah spoke to the nobles, the leaders, those in positions of influence, and then he spoke to the rest of the people. Notice the trickledown effect. If the leaders wouldn't buy in to the vision, if they would not shift their focus to the work of God, then the rest of the people would never do so. Nehemiah's instruction to them was do not be afraid. Remember the Lord who is great and awesome and fight for your brethren, your sons, and your daughters.

Let's look at each point Nehemiah made. First of all, he told them to not be afraid. In the Word of God, every major victory God orchestrates is preceded by a message to His children to "fear not." We have to first overcome fear so that we can remember God who is great and awesome. We have to stop fearing the circumstances and the threats around us and realize Who called us, Who is able to keep us and Who is able to preserve the seed that has been planted in us.

Next, he told them to fight. Once we have remembered the Lord who is mighty in power, we can fight for our brethren, our sons, our daughters, our wives and our homes. If your vision is just big enough for one, then it's not a God vision. God's vision always involves connecting with people. When we first saw Nehemiah, he had just learned of a need. He wept when he heard of the destruction of Jerusalem, that the walls were down and the gates were burned. Concern gripped his heart. No doubt he thought of the sons, the daughters, the wives of Jerusalem. A vision was birthed in him to assist these people in rising above the struggle to rebuild what had been destroyed. This is the vision he would cast. It was a vision that would benefit many of God's people.

Many times when our dreams are under fire, we begin to second-guess what God has called us to do. We begin to think that maybe we don't have what it takes. Maybe we're wasting our time. Maybe nobody will come alongside us. These are the thoughts we must subdue if we are to move ahead. Sanballat made some valid points in his arguments. Sanballat said the walls would not hold, they would not be strong enough. He said there was not enough people for such a large undertaking. He said there was too much rubble to dig through. These were valid points. What he was saying made natural sense, but not necessarily spiritual sense. Sometimes well-meaning people make valid points, but they are not leaving room for God in the equation. Nehemiah was responding to what God had put in his heart. Most divine visions are impossible. Most visions would never hold up to a feasibility study. But only when you don't factor in God.

When Anne and I were called of the Lord to plant Livingway Family Church in Brownsville, we didn't do a feasibility study. We didn't take a poll to see who was with us. We stepped out in faith, burned all bridges and determined that sink or swim, we were going to be fully devoted to God. For much of what we were called to do, we did not have the skill, ability, finances or education to complete

Innovation

it. But we committed ourselves to remembering the ways God intervened for us early on. I think of David's example in 1 Samuel 17:34-37. David was preparing to go out into battle against a much bigger opponent, Goliath. As David stood before Saul, he began remembering aloud all the times God was with him as he faced lions, bears, and other predators while tending his father's sheep. David concluded by saying that just as God had delivered him from all of those, He would be with him and enable him to overcome the great Philistine giant Goliath. Just as David did, we can draw strength and momentum from past victories.

On one of our recent fishing trips, two gentlemen from the church joined us. One of the gentlemen knew the area better than I did so we allowed him to guide us and tell us where to fish that day. When we got to the location, because I'd never fished there before, my confidence was at a minimum. A number of thoughts clouded my mind: *This is the wrong spot. The water is too rough. The bait is wrong. The color of the lures is wrong.* As I was entertaining these thoughts, all of a sudden the gentleman who was guiding us hooked the biggest fish we had ever brought on our boat - a black drum weighing in at over 35 pounds.

It's so easy to be critical of the unknown. When we find ourselves in a unknown land, we feel awkward and off our game. It is in these situations where our critics live and breathe. When you find yourself facing the unknown, go back and read the scriptures the Lord gave you at the beginning of your journey. Sometimes we forget our roots. We forget where God has brought us from. We have to go back and visit those things that God has spoken to us before so that we can continue to move forward. In times like these, we must remember the Lord who is great and awesome.

The third thing the example of Nehemiah teaches us to do when faced with adversity is revise the plan. Consider the words of Nehemiah 4:9: "Nevertheless we made our prayer to our God, and because of them we set a watch against them day and night" (NKJV). Up until this particular season of adversity, Nehemiah and the Israelites had followed one plan. But this change in circumstances called for a change in plan. It called for God's people to be creative and adapt. Now they would set a watch. The vision didn't change, but the plan had to be revised.

Walking by faith does not preclude leading strategically. Nehemiah 4:16-18 tells of Nehemiah's strategy: "So it was, from that time on, that half of my servants worked at construction, while the other half held the spears, the shields, the bows, and wore armor; and the leaders were behind all the house of Judah. Those who built on the wall, and those who carried burdens, loaded themselves so that with one hand they worked at construction, and with the other held a weapon. Every one of the builders had his sword girded at his side as he built. And the one who sounded the trumpet was beside me" (NKJV).

That's innovation at its best! The vision of rebuilding the walls never changed, but the plan to get the job done was constantly evolving. Nehemiah and those who worked with him changed strategy in that now one half would hold the tools of building while the other half held instruments of war. One half would hold off the enemy while the other half would build what God called them to build. That's innovative management. Never confuse plans with God's vision. Plans may fail, but the vision will not fail. Plans are simply a means to the fulfillment of the vision. It's easy to lose sight of the vision when plans fail, but just because situations change, don't resort to withdraw. Determine to press on and get God's plan for the moment. Keep your mind and emotions in check to avoid drifting into the realm of unbelief and doubt.

There are times when circumstances will call for a visionary to swallow his pride and revise his initial plan. Sadly, there are businesses that no longer exist today and ministries that are struggling because of the "P" word. Their pride is too great to enable them to make a change. The need to change plans does not indicate a failure on the part of the leader; it is simply a necessary reaction in response to changing circumstances. The best laid plans are often revised.

It has been said whenever you ask God for a miracle, He will instruct you to do something. Such was the case with Nehemiah. He had to follow the instructional voice of God. God was using him to solve a problem. Nehemiah would finish the project because he was a problem solver with an innovative spirit. In life, your rewards are often determined by the problems you solve for others.

Nehemiah's enemies tried to thwart the rebuilding efforts by threatening military action. This initially caused insurrection among the Jews working alongside Nehemiah. But Nehemiah's perseverance and innovation refocused the people as he modified the plan, which made them feel more secure in their environment. As they prayed and looked to God and were reminded why they were rebuilding the wall in the first place, the project was able to continue. And what happened to Israel's enemies when work continued? Nehemiah 4:15 tells us: "And it happened, when our enemies heard that it was known to us, and that God had brought their plot to nothing, that all of us returned to the wall, everyone to his work" (NKJV). Work continued. Israel's enemies knew that God had brought their schemes to nothing. You see, visions may refine, but they don't change. The work proceeded according to the vision God had given Nehemiah.

When faced with adversity, a successful leader will follow the example of Nehemiah. He will pray. He will remember what God has done in the past. He will revise his plans as necessary. And then, just as Nehemiah experienced, he will continue to successfully pursue the vision that God has placed in his heart.

Innovation

Chapter Fifteen
Open Heavens

In his book on vision, Myles Monroe relates a story about Walt Disney. Shortly after Walt Disney World opened, they had only one ride in the park. One day, Walt Disney was sitting on a bench in the park, just staring into space – or so it seemed. One of his workers who was manicuring the grass came past and asked, "How are you, sir?"

Without looking at the man, Disney said, "Fine," and kept on staring.

The worker then asked, "Mr. Disney, what are you doing?"

"I'm looking at my mountain," Disney answered. "I see the mountain right there." Walt later described this mountain to his architects and they drew up the plans based on Walt's vision.

Disney died before construction on Space Mountain was completed. On the day the ride was dedicated, the governor and the mayor were present, as was Disney's widow. One of the young men in attendance at the dedication stood to introduce Mrs. Disney and said, "It's a pity that Mr. Walt Disney is not here today to see this mountain, but we're glad his wife is here."

Mrs. Disney walked up to the podium, looked at the crowd and said, "In fact, I must correct this young man. Walt already saw the mountain. It is you who are just now seeing it." Never underestimate the power of vision to bring about great things.

Consider this exchange between Jesus and His disciples found in Matthew 16:13-19:

"When Jesus came into the region of Caesarea Philippi, He asked His disciples, saying, 'Who do men say that I, the Son of Man, am?'

"So they said, 'Some say John the Baptist, some Elijah, and others Jeremiah or one of the prophets.'

"He said to them, 'But who do you say that I am?'

"Simon Peter answered and said, 'You are the Christ, the Son of the living God.'

"Jesus answered and said to him, 'Blessed are you, Simon Bar-Jonah, for flesh and blood has not revealed this to you, but My Father who is in heaven. And I also say to you that you are Peter, and on this rock I will build My church, and the gates of Hades shall not prevail against it. And I will give you the keys of the kingdom of heaven, and whatever you bind on earth will be bound in heaven, and whatever you loose on earth will be loosed in heaven'" (NKJV).

Many times as leaders and innovators, we tend to focus not on the one who has a revelation of who we are or who is able to affirm our leadership skills or abilities, but we tend to focus on what the others are not saying. Sometimes, silence is deafening. It's not the affirmation of the one, it's the silence of the 11 that affects many leaders. Especially as pastors, sometimes we tend to look at those who are not with us rather than those who are with us, those who stayed home from church rather than those who showed up to show their support, those who gave in a special offering rather than those who gave all. We tend to focus on those who didn't say thank you during pastor's appreciation offering rather than those who showed up and voiced their support. The silence of those who say nothing at all has crippled the hearts of many leaders.

God can do amazing things with the belief of just one. He started with just one man, Adam, and brought forth all mankind. He took one man, Abraham, and though he and his wife were up in years, He made him the father of many nations. He took a prostitute named Rahab and used her as a strategic partner for Joshua to conquer Jericho. In John 12, we read about the impact that Lazarus had on an entire city. People heard about what Jesus had done in his life and many believed. This is the power of one. Peter spoke the revelation that God had given him – that Jesus was the Christ. Jesus told Peter that because of his confession – the confession of one – he would receive the keys to the kingdom. Never underestimate the power of one life, the power of one revelation, the power of one confession. God will open the heavens for just one.

God caused the heavens to open for Jacob. In Genesis 28:10-22, we see Jacob stop for the night in Bethel and lay his head on a rock, tired and hungry. As he slept, he had a vision of angels descending and ascending a ladder and he heard the voice of God.

Jacob realized he had been given a glimpse into the heavens and he set up a monument to memorialize the place where God had opened the heavens just for him.

The heavens opened for Enoch and he was taken home to be with God because he walked with God in righteousness (Genesis 5:24). Elijah saw the heavens open and he was taken up in a chariot of fire because of the anointing that was upon his life (2 Kings 2:11). Paul tells us that he was caught up to the third heaven and saw things that were not lawful to be uttered (2 Corinthians 12:3-6). Heaven was opened for him because of his faithfulness. John was in the Spirit on the Lord's day when the heavens opened and he was given a vision of the end of the age (Revelation 1).

Consider this account of the early church, found Acts 4:32-33: "Now the multitude of those who believed were of one heart and one soul; neither did anyone say that any of the things he possessed was his own, but they had all things in common. And with great power the apostles gave witness to the resurrection of the Lord Jesus. And great grace was upon them all" (NKJV). The believers experienced power and grace because of their response to God. Their giving opened the heavens.

God's grace empowers us to go beyond our natural ability. The Greek word translated "favor" is *carateo*, which means to be drawn. The position of our heart determines the measure of favor and grace that we receive. We must position ourselves in such a way that we can be drawn to God and experience His grace. God's voice will tell us which way to go so that we can be positioned to receive His supernatural provision.

Grace flows through our connection with Jesus Christ and the strength of our connection to Christ is determined by our obedience to God. As we walk in His righteousness in full obedience to the Father, Romans 5:17 declares that we receive an abundance of grace through our Lord Jesus Christ. Through Him, we reign in life as kings.

Finis Dake said, "Here is the true observance of Christian love, that is to live solely for others instead of ourselves." As we love God and love others, we literally open the windows of heaven. Remember, innovators are always concerned about including others in pursuit of the vision. If your vision is just big enough for you, then it is not a God-sized vision. God gives us a heart of compassion to accompany the vision He places in our hearts.

Consider the example of Barnabas found in Acts 4:36-37: "And Joses, who was also named Barnabas by the apostles (which is translated Son of Encouragement), a Levite of the country of Cyprus, having land, sold it, and brought the money and laid it at the apostles' feet" (NKJV). It was no accident that the early church took in Joses, a man from Cyprus who most believe was converted on the day of Pentecost when Peter preached the gospel and that first 3,000 men were saved for the kingdom of God. Barnabas was taken in by the church and he found his identity in the fellowship of other godly individuals. They rightfully named him "son of encouragement" because he constantly encouraged others by his gifts. His life became an outpouring of encouragement as he gave whatever he had to benefit others.

God has called us to be problem solvers. Usually, what infuriates us on the inside is a problem that God has called us to solve. Those things that strongly affect us can often be good indicators of our God-given assignment on the earth. God has called us to innovate that others might be delivered. He has called us to alleviate grief through our acts of obedience. He has called us to sow seeds in the kingdom of God on a regular basis by being a giver in our local church. As we faithfully do these things, the windows of heaven open over our lives so that God can share insights that bring greater blessing.

As we give of ourselves and our resources, the windows of heaven open. Spiritual rain falls upon our lives. When we speak of open windows, we often focus on material blessings. It is true that God can bless us with all we need physically, but do not limit God to simply physical provision. The currency of heaven is revelation. As God opens the windows of heaven, He pours forth revelation for innovation so that His people can be on the cutting edge and walk in all the fullness He intends for us. Revelation is what brings transformation to our lives and a manifestation of God's power.

When you are living under an open heaven, you have access to truths that others cannot imagine. As with Peter's confession of Jesus as the Christ, flesh and blood didn't bring that revelation. God revealed that truth to Peter. We understand that the more we submit to God, the more the Spirit of truth can dwell in us and make us free. The more the Spirit of truth reveals the true nature of God to us, the easier it is submit to His leadership. It's a beautiful cycle that can change your destiny forever.

In Numbers 13, we read that Moses sent spies out into Canaan.

Canaan represented a good land of abundance and prosperity. Moses sent out these spies with instructions to thoroughly investigate the land. When the spies returned, they brought a bad report. Numbers 13:33 gives the report of the majority of the spies: "There we saw the giants (the descendants of Anak came from the giants); and we were like grasshoppers in our own sight, and so we were in their sight" (NKJV). Based upon the report of these spies, the children of Israel decided not to enter Canaan and instead, spent many years wandering in the wilderness.

Fast-forward forty years. Joshua is now the leader of Israel, following the death of Moses. The children of Israel come to the edge of the Promised Land and Joshua sends spies to evaluate the situation. In Joshua 2:23-24, we see that these spies came back with a completely different report. They returned and said to Joshua, "Truly the Lord has delivered all the land into our hands, for indeed all the inhabitants of the country are fainthearted because of us" (Joshua 2:24, NKJV). Joshua led the Israelites into Canaan and they immediately took the city of Jericho, en route to taking the entire Promised Land.

What can we learn from these two examples? Innovators do their research, but they always view their findings with divine optimism. Never forget, it's how you see the land that determines your potential for taking the land. The outlook of the spies determined everything about their future. Likewise, it matters little how the enemy sees you; your success in battle is determined by how you see your enemy. Through the power of vision, we can bring our enemy down to size. If we allow ourselves to see things through God's eyes, we can shrink our giants and remove any mountains that might attempt to stand in our way.

In First Samuel 30, David and his mighty men had just returned from fighting to their home in Ziklag. When they got there, they found that the city had been burned and their families had been taken. The things that were most precious to them appeared to be lost. Many of you are reading this book on innovation out of desperation because the things you held most dear have been taken and try as you may, you cannot figure out how to get them back. The Bible tells us that when David was faced with this situation, called for an ephod, which is a priestly garment. He then began to seek the Lord, even though his heart was broken. The first step to your recovery is the same - call for your priestly garments and begin to seek the face of God. When David called upon the Lord, God answered him. When you begin to look for God to open the windows of heaven, calling upon the name of the Lord, the heavens will open and God will speak to your situation.

As David sought the Lord in praise, God told him to pursue his enemies. The Lord assured him he would overtake his enemies and recover all. So many times, when we get a word, we sit on the word rather than act. The Lord told David to pursue. David didn't know exactly what direction to go in, but he began to amass a group of men to go with him on the journey. Two hundred men were too tired from the previous battle, but four hundred did engage with him and took off on the journey. It's amazing how movement creates moments in the Spirit. Nothing happens until we decide to move in response to the prompting of God. When we begin to act

- we sow a seed, we make a phone call, we take a step of obedience, we continue through adversity, we continue to attend church and serve others - God gets involved in our process.

The Bible tells us in 1 Samuel 30:11-12, "Then they found an Egyptian in the field, and brought him to David; and they gave him bread and he ate, and they let him drink water. And they gave him a piece of a cake of figs and two clusters of raisins. So when he had eaten, his strength came back to him; for he had eaten no bread nor drunk water for three days and three nights" (NKJV). Some of you reading this have yet to find your Egyptian but believe me, God has placed one there. Somewhere in your life, if you respond in obedience to God, you will find your own Egyptian who will take you to the place where you will recover all you have lost. This Egyptian represented David's opportunity. David had an opportunity to treat this Egyptian with kindness and care for his needs. He could have viewed him as the enemy. He could have accused him of lighting the match to burn down the houses and carry off the families of his men, but that was not how David responded.

As David and his men ministered to the needs of this Egyptian man, the windows of heaven were opened. The man shared classified information that would aid David and his men in the recovery of their families from the hands of the Amalekites. First Samuel 30:18-19 tells us, "So David recovered all that the Amalekites had carried away, and David rescued his two wives. And nothing of theirs was lacking, either small or great, sons or daughters, spoil or anything which they had taken from them; David recovered

Innovation

all" (NKJV).

We have an opportunity to sow a seed in the life of another. We have an opportunity to be blessed through an act of obedience.

Today, God wants you to recover everything that you've lost. He wants to open the heavens. We are told that nothing of theirs was lacking; David and his men recovered everything. When you follow God in obedience and live under an open heaven, nothing will be lacking in your life - not in your family, your job, or your relationships. There will be nothing wasted because you are following God's plan for your life.

I heard a story about a young man who received his driver's license and that summer, he began to ask his parents when he could get a car. He didn't care what kind of car it was. For many of us, if our first car was a tin box with wheels, we would have gladly driven it. This young man just wanted a car.

He began to bug his dad daily, asking when he would get a car. His dad said, "I want you to take this book and read it. When you've read the book, come back to me and we'll talk about the car."

The young man threw the book on his nightstand. About a week later, he again asked his dad if they could talk about getting him a car. His dad asked, "Have you read the book yet?"

The young man replied, "No. But I looked at it."

The dad said, "Well, when you read the book, we'll talk about the car."

Another week went by and the young man continued to probe

his dad for the car he desired. Again the dad asked, "Have you read the book?"

The young man said, "Well, I opened the book. I looked inside. It has pages with words on them."

The dad said, "When you read the book, then I'll talk to you about the car."

Finally, summer was coming to a close. The young man, in desperation, said, "Dad, please, when are we going to get my car?"

The dad said, "I know you've obviously not read the book. Get the book and bring it to me now." When the young man handed the book to his dad, his dad turned to the back of the book where he had written a paragraph. He gave the book back to the young man and said, "Read this."

The young man read what his father had written: "Son, your mom and I bought you a car. The keys are in my pocket. The car is parked at the neighbor's. Thanks for being obedient and reading the book like I asked you to."

The irony is that the young man had wasted an entire summer because he failed to be obedient to his father's instruction to read the book. How much of our lives have been wasted because we failed to respond to God's instruction? Our obedience opens the heavens over our jobs, our families, our church, our ministries, our children, and so much more. Unimagined blessing is just one act of obedience away. Open the heavens and make it rain.

Innovation

Chapter Sixteen
Favor for the Moment

Sometimes we look at people who are extremely talented in certain areas such as sports, music or acting, or maybe they are gifted in areas of academia or business, and we talk about how they make what they do look effortless. The mark of a man or woman who has favor on their life is that they are able to do what God called them to do with ease because favor makes everything easier.

Second Corinthians 6:2 says, "For he says, 'In the time of my favor I heard you, and in the day of salvation I helped you.' I tell you, now is the time of God's favor, now is the day of salvation" (NIV). As a God-anointed innovator, we must believe that the favor of God is on us. God's favor makes us irresistible. This scripture makes it clear that now is the time of God's favor. A visitation of favor precedes a visitation of salvation, which means that now is the day of salvation.

Consider this exchange between Mary and the angel, found in Luke 1:28-30: "The angel went to her and said, 'Greetings, you who are highly favored! The Lord is with you.' Mary was greatly troubled at his words and wondered what kind of greeting this might be. But the angel said to her, 'Do not be afraid, Mary; you have found favor with God'" (NIV).

Don't be taken aback by a declaration of God's favor over your life. Everything starts with the acceptance of God's blessing. Do you know that you are uniquely blessed of God? You say, well I don't feel blessed. Those who discount their blessing tend to judge themselves in the light of other people's blessing. Comparison will always lead to deception. If you got out of bed this morning, you're blessed. If you had a roof over your head, you're blessed. If you put two feet on the ground and walked forward, you're blessed. If you had a job to go to, you're blessed. If you have ears to hear and eyes to see, you're blessed. If you have a nose to smell chocolate chip cookies baking in the oven, you're blessed.

Our middle son, Marcus, lives in Austin. When he comes home to visit, you know he is in the house because the smell of chocolate chips permeates the entire house. When I think of chocolate chips, I think of Marcus, and when I think of Marcus, I remember how blessed I am. We are blessed people. Sometimes, we fail to count the little blessings, but if we did, we'd realize how blessed we truly are. God's blessing is upon each of us.

Sometimes, we expect to be rejected. This should not be. The favor of God is upon our life and if God is for us, who can be against us? Nothing is impossible with God.

Recently, our church wanted to put up an advertisement at a bus stop by our local mall. Before I inquired about the possibility, I felt defeated. I assumed that because of the great location of the billboard, it wouldn't be available. I even thought, *I don't know why I'm calling because I know someone has already reserved that space.* I had to overcome my certainty of rejection and remember the favor of God instead. Once I did that, I was able to call and found out that it was indeed available. That turned out to be one of the greatest types of advertising we had ever done because everybody who visited the mall was able to see the banner and receive current information about our church.

We have to begin to expect the favor of God to abound in our lives and reject the feelings of inadequacy the enemy will send our way. Perhaps you've heard the story about Sam and the duck. When Sam was eleven, he and his sister loved to visit their grandparents. While at their grandparents' house in the country, Sam would go outside with his BB gun and shoot cans.

One day, Sam was walking back to the house for lunch and he spotted his grandma's old duck in the pond. He thought surely he could never hit the duck with his BB gun so just for fun, he drew aim and fired away. Much to his chagrin, he hit the duck square between the eyes and killed his grandma's old duck. Looking around, he saw that apparently no one had seen what had happened. Sam quickly took the duck from the water and buried it, then went inside for lunch.

Innovation

Sam felt tremendous guilt, but that wasn't the worst of it. As it turned out, his sister had seen him shoot the duck and then hide the duck's body – and she told him she knew what he had done. When lunch was over and it was time to wash the dishes and do the other chores, Grandmother called on Sissy to do the work, but Sissy said, "Oh, Sam wants to do the dishes and take the trash out today." As Sissy walked by Sam, she whispered in his ear, "Remember the duck." Sam quietly went about his chores while Sissy played outside.

The next day, Grandpa had planned a fishing trip. He asked Sam if he was ready to go when Sissy said, "Sam decided that he would stay home today and be with Grandmother while I go fishing with you." As she walked by Sam, she whispered in his ear, "Remember the duck."

Later on that evening, Sam couldn't take it any longer. He burst into the kitchen where Grandmother was doing the dishes and said, "Grandma, I have to confess. I aimed at your duck, even though I didn't think I could hit him with my gun, and accidentally killed the old duck."

Grandmother said, "Don't worry about it. I saw it all out the kitchen window. I just wondered how long you were going to let your sister hold that over your head." All too often we go through life like Sam, allowing the enemy to hold things over our head. Instead, we should claim the forgiveness and mercy of God and the favor of God and then move on with our lives.

Luke 2:52 says, "And Jesus grew in wisdom and stature, and in favor with God and man" (NIV). This scripture seems to indicate that we can grow or increase in favor. Likewise, if we continue in disobedience, we can lose the favor of God. Consider the example of King Saul. He started his administration in the favor of God, but through repeated disobedience, he reached a point where he lost the favor of God and lost his position as king. Daniel, however, enjoyed exceptional favor upon his entire life because he obeyed God and had an extraordinary spirit. Your spirit can become extraordinary with the inundation of God's presence and glory.

Favor is evidence that God likes us. Do not misunderstand – God loves all humanity. John 3:16 reminds us that God so loved the world that He gave His Son. God loves the sinner, but we have found favor in His sight. Consider these words from Ephesians 2:7-8: "He did this that He might clearly demonstrate through the ages to come the immeasurable (limitless, surpassing) riches of His free grace (His unmerited favor) in [His] kindness and goodness of heart toward us in Christ Jesus. For it is by free grace (God's unmerited favor) that you are saved (delivered from judgment and made partakers of Christ's salvation) through [your] faith. And this [salvation] is not of yourselves [of your own doing, it came not through your own striving], but it is the gift of God" (AMP).

God's favor is a gift given to us. God's favor is exhibited in the riches of His kindness and goodness of heart toward us which He promises to demonstrate through the ages. It is more than just the salvation of our souls or forgiveness of sins; God's extravagant love toward us also includes the limitless, unsurpassed riches of His kindness and mercy. God oftentimes blesses us in simple ways to evidence the fact that He's thinking about us.

Innovation

Awhile back, I was thinking about a particular Christian artist whose music I hadn't heard in a long time. I used to have some of their CD's, but had misplaced all of them. No sooner had this thought passed through my head, than someone in our church – who had no idea what I had been thinking - came to me and brought me three of that artist's CD's. I thought, *What a revelation of God's love!* God had me on His mind and sought to bless me, even without my asking.

If we're constantly rehearsing everything that is wrong in our lives and reminding God of all the problems we are experiencing, it won't draw God near to us. In fact, such constant badgering is a cloak of unbelief. But when we rehearse God's Word, calling Him to remember what He said, it brings Him joy. He loves to hear us speak His Word. He loves to hear His children claim His promises. That brings His favor.

If you are a parent, you don't want your children constantly reminding you that you need to go to the store to buy supplies for their school project. If they are constantly reminding you of their needs, you have a propensity to react negatively. But if they make their request for supplies and then rest, knowing that you will get them what they need, your attitude will be completely different. When they frame their request properly and with the right attitude, it's amazing how it draws you in and makes you determined to get what they need. It makes you want to provide for them. If we, as imperfect human parents, feel this way, how much more so would God want to provide for His children? He has the perfect Father's heart. He hears us when we call and responds to those who remember and rehearse His promises in His ear.

There is great power in a blessing. On Friday evenings in orthodox Jewish homes, the father lays his hands on his children and pronounces God's blessing over them. No wonder Jewish children grow up to be winners in life! Jews have become some of the world's greatest inventors, bankers, musicians, and entertainers. Although a minority race, the Jews have produced an astonishing number of Nobel Prize winners. I believe this is because they bless their children in the same way the patriarchs of the Old Testament did. Abraham, Isaac and Jacob released God's blessing upon their children by laying hands on them and speaking forth blessings (Genesis 27, 49). In the New Testament, the apostles pronounced blessings over the churches in which they ministered and the believers who stood alongside them. Over the church in Philippi, Paul declared, "And my God shall supply all your need according to His riches in glory by Christ Jesus" (Philippians 4:19, NKJV). John released a powerful blessing upon Gaius when he said, "Beloved, I pray that you may prosper in all things and be in health, just as your soul prospers" (3 John 1:2, NKJV).

Those who walk in favor should declare it every day. Every day we should speak to release the favor of God over our lives. We should declare open heavens for our families and ourselves. We must declare all debts cancelled. We must declare the curse is broken. We must declare our children are kept, saved, healed, and filled by the power of the blood. We must understand that death and life are in the power of our tongue and blessings are procured and enforced through the spoken word (Proverbs 18:21).

Innovation

We cannot keep silent when it comes to declaring the blessing of God over our lives. To walk in favor is to first understand the unique blessing that abides on your life. Understand that the Word of God says we have been blessed with all spiritual blessings in Christ Jesus (Ephesians 1:3). Some people don't see themselves as blessed. But truthfully, we don't realize how blessed we are until we stop and evaluate our blessings. We must not keep silent concerning God's favor on our life. It must be spoken to have life.

Bill and his wife Blanche went to the state fair every year. Every year Bill would say, "Blanche, I'd like to ride that helicopter ride," to which Blanche would reply, "I know Bill, but that helicopter ride costs fifty bucks and fifty bucks is fifty bucks."

One year, Bill and Blanche went to the fair and Bill said, "Blanche, I'm 75 years old. If I don't ride that helicopter ride, I might never get another chance to do it."

Blanche replied, "Bill, that helicopter ride is fifty bucks and fifty bucks is fifty bucks."

The pilot overheard the couple and said, "Folks, I'll make you a deal. I'll take both of you for a ride if you can stay quiet for the entire ride and not say a word. I won't charge you a penny, but if you say one word, it's fifty dollars."

Bill and Blanche agreed and up they went. The pilot did all kinds of fancy maneuvers, but not a word was heard. He did his best daredevil tricks over and over again, but still, not a word was uttered. When they landed, the pilot turned to Bill and said, "By golly. I did everything I could do to get you to yell out, but you didn't. I'm impressed."

Bill replied, "Well, to tell you the truth, I almost said something when Blanche fell out. But you know, fifty bucks is fifty bucks."

When it comes to favor, we can't stay quiet. We must speak the revelation that we've received if we ever expect it to manifest. There's a sequence to manifestation. Revelation leads to illumination. Illumination leads to transformation. Transformation then leads to the manifestation of blessing in our lives.

Innovation

Chapter Seventeen
Favor the Elevator

The story of Queen Esther is a classic example of how favor gives your life distinction. Esther was a young Jewish girl living in Persia during the reign of King Xerxes. King Xerxes was looking for a new queen and Esther was one of those taken to the palace for consideration. Let's pick up Esther's story in Esther 2:17: "The king loved Esther more than all the other women, and she obtained grace and favor in his sight more than all the virgins; so he set the royal crown upon her head and made her queen instead of Vashti" (NKJV).

It doesn't matter how many haters you have in your life; when favor is on you, it'll elevate you head and shoulders above your peers. Favor is the extra muscle we need to accomplish what God has put in our heart. Favor will cause us to walk in the full potential of God's anointing upon our lives. Esther was an orphan living in a strange land with her uncle Mordecai. But God used Mordecai as

Innovation

a mentor in Esther's life. Mordecai was the one who helped Esther prepare for the palace. Mordecai didn't see where Esther was, he saw where she was going. He had a vision of greatness for Esther, just like God has a vision of greatness for us. Just as Mordecai assisted Esther, the Holy Spirit works in our life to remind us of our place and position in God.

When Esther and the other young ladies arrived at the palace, they were put through a year of beauty treatments. They were polished, purified and made ready to see the king. God will also take you through a process of adornment and purification. Esther allowed herself to be polished and made ready and she found favor with the king. We're all on a quest for access. Even aliens can become intimates when favor is upon their life.

Sometimes finding favor involves a process of study and analysis. God gave Esther the wisdom to position herself for favor. She had the same innovative spirit that God gives to all those who call upon His name. Just as we found in the case of Daniel, Esther had an extraordinary spirit. Everything in our life follows our spirit. Our body, our finances, our creativity - they all follow the spirit. The condition of our spirit determines how far our favor will take us. Esther surpassed all the others, not because she did more, but because she was more.

But we also know that Esther was not elevated by God's favor to this position for no reason. You see in the process of time, Mordecai offended one of the king's top men, Haman, when he refused to bow down to him. Haman was so incensed, he convinced the king to issue a decree that all the Jews be destroyed. When Mordecai learned of the plot, he knew he had to tell Esther about it. At first, Esther was not sure what she could do to change the course. For anyone to approach the king without and invitation could mean death for them, and the king had not invited Esther into his presence for some time. But Mordecai reminded Esther that she had an obligation to act because of the favor she had been shown by God. In Esther 4:14 he said these words, "Who knows whether you have come to the kingdom for such a time as this?" (NKJV). Favor is about strategic placement. Favor will position us where we can do the most good for the people God has assigned us to.

Haman's plan was still in place to destroy the Jews and he prepared a gallows on which he planned to hang Mordecai and the others. Esther, knowing that it could mean her death, boldly requested an audience with the king. The king welcomed Esther into his presence and when Esther told him of Haman's horrible plot, the king turned the tables on Haman and hanged him on the very gallows he had constructed for his enemies, the Jews. Esther found favor with the king and saved a nation in the process.

God revealed His greatness as He positioned Esther for favor. We, too, are positioned for favor that we might see the great hand of God. Consider these words from Psalm 102:13 and 16: "You will arise and have mercy on Zion; For the time to favor her, Yes, the set time, has come. For the LORD shall build up Zion; He shall appear in His glory" (NKJV).

God builds His church with favor. We are the body of Christ. God builds our lives and positions us for revelations of His greatness in our lives. At every stage of our journey, God reveals His favor.

He reveals His goodness and mercy to strengthen us along the way.

It's been said that favor is what happens when preparation meets opportunity. Esther had prepared her heart for this moment. She, like so many of us, didn't realize the full measure of favor upon her life. It is favor that opens the doors, changes the hearts of kings, and saves nations. Do not misunderstand. Favor does not mean that everyone will like you, just those people who are critical to open the doors of destiny for your life. Your destiny is not in the hands of man. Your destiny is in the hands of God, who is able to open the doors with the right people to cause you to be ushered in to opportunity and blessing.

King David had favor with those with whom he needed favor, even though he was unrecognized and forgotten as a young shepherd in his father's house. When Samuel went to Jesse's house to anoint the next king of Israel, he was tempted to select one of David's older brothers. But Samuel was checked in spirit and reminded that God had someone else in mind. Sameul called on Jesse to bring his young son from obscurity so he could be anointed and set apart because favor was upon his life. You don't have to be the biggest or most powerful, you just need the force of favor in your life.

Daniel found favor with the administrations of Nebuchadnezzar and Darius. The Bible tells us in Daniel 6:28, that he prospered. Joseph found favor at Potiphar's house. Moses had favor before Pharaoh. Mordecai experienced favor as he was transported from mourning on a pile of ashes to being celebrated while wearing the king's robes and riding the king's war horse through the city. Favor can restore in a day what was stolen over a lifetime. Psalm 5:12 says, "For You, O Lord, will bless the righteous; With favor You will surround him as with a shield" (NKJV).

I remember the testimony of a couple in our church. The husband had been unemployed for quite some time, but when they heard the message on favor and how tithing and obedience release the favor of God, they determined to stay obedient to God through the lean times. They shared with us that God turned their circumstances around in one week's time. They received not only a job, but also a healthy signing bonus. A settlement that had been outstanding for months was reached, the house that they couldn't rent for months was able to be rented and a wire transfer to their account was found that they had totally forgotten about. Favor can turn your life around in one day's time.

Favor is that hidden ingredient that we often fail to factor into our life struggles. Psalm 119:58 says, "I entreated Your favor with my whole heart; Be merciful to me according to Your word" (NKJV). In other words, we are told to ask God for His favor. Ask God for that good parking space up in front. Ask God for those good seats. Ask God to give you favor at work. Ask God to give you favor to find good deals, increase your finances and stretch your money. Ask God and He will answer. When we ask, we need to expect God to put favor on us so key people will have a favorable disposition towards us. The Bible said of Abraham that he didn't stagger at the promise of God. He didn't stagger at the measure of favor that God had promised him. We have to wrap our hearts and our heads around the goodness of God and embrace it.

Innovation

Think of the experience of Mary and Joseph. When Jesus was born, they were in Bethlehem staying in a stable, as there was no room for them in the inn. When they went to the temple to present Jesus for the first time, they did not have enough material resources to present the standard offering of a lamb. Instead, they offered a poor person's offering consisting of two turtledoves and a young pigeon. Mary and Joseph were not wealthy by the world's standards, but God's favor was most definitely on them and God provided. Consider the account of the visit of the wise men found in Matthew 2:11, "And when they had come into the house, they saw the young Child with Mary His mother, and fell down and worshiped Him. And when they had opened their treasures, they presented gifts to Him: gold, frankincense, and myrrh" (NKJV). God knew that Mary and Joseph would have to make an exodus to Egypt with their young child, so God provided for the journey that was ahead.

Contrary to popular belief, Jesus didn't live as a pauper. How do you pay for a staff of twelve, their families and the rest of the ministry team if you are a pauper? He had everything He needed. Jesus had a treasury. He often told His followers to give the surplus to the poor. When Jesus was crucified, they took His garment and cast lots for it because it was equivalent in value to a modern day Armani suit. Jesus did not live an ostentatious life, but He certainly did have more than enough to take care of His needs and the needs of His friends and followers.

Favor has that effect on your life. God provided for Israel when they left Egypt after 400-plus years in slavery. He made the

Favor the Elevator

Egyptians favorably disposed toward them so they left slavery with the riches of Egypt in their packs. God provided for Jesus, Mary and Joseph knowing that they would have to travel to Egypt to seek refuge. In the same way, God will bless you in your coming in and in your going out. We are a generation living under an outpouring of God's favor.

Genesis 39:2-4 tells a bit of the story of Joseph: "The LORD was with Joseph, and he was a successful man; and he was in the house of his master the Egyptian. And his master saw that the LORD was with him and that the LORD made all he did to prosper in his hand. So Joseph found favor in his sight, and served him. Then he made him overseer of his house, and all that he had he put under his authority" (NKJV).

Whatever Joseph did prospered because the Lord was with him. When God is with you, you appear better than you really are. His presence is the great equalizer. His favor is what causes others to like you and open doors of prosperity towards you.

There are many prophetic parallels between the nation of Israel and the body of Christ (the Church). We see Pharaoh as the anti-Christ. We can see Goshen as a precursor of the kingdom of God. We see Egypt as the world's system. The plagues represent the power of God coming down to break demonic strongholds that have ruled the earth for thousands of years. God opened the Red Sea for the Israelites to walk through to safety, just as He shed His Son's blood that we might come through the blood to salvation. Just as the pillar of cloud and pillar of fire led the Israelites to the Promised Land, so the Holy Ghost provides leadership in our lives today.

Innovation

Also, just as the Israelites suffered in bondage, often we who are living under God's favor experience adversity. Consider these words from Exodus 1:11, "Therefore they set taskmasters over them to afflict them with their burdens. And they built for Pharaoh supply cities, Pithom and Raamses" (NKJV).

The Israelites were forced to build these massive supply cities for Pharaoh. They were building up the economic dynasty of their vicious taskmaster. Many of God's people today feel like they are in bondage to the world's financial system. I spoke to a businessman recently who said, "I'm tired of seeing the world out-prosper the people of God, outshine, and outdo God's people. They're flying in the jets and we're driving in our cars." Jesus said that the children of this world are wiser than the children of light. The children of this world often put all their focus and energy behind prospering materially. As children of light, we understand that there is more to life than just making money. But shouldn't we be able to excel with the favor and grace of God upon our lives?

Exodus 1:13 says, "So the Egyptians made the children of Israel serve with rigor" (NKJV). The Egyptians were hard taskmasters. And as if that was not enough, in the midst of their hardships, Pharaoh ordered the murder of all the newborn Hebrew males. Satan doesn't want a generation of deliverers to be birthed, so he tries to stop each one of us as he tried to stop Moses in the Old Testament. Satan wants to use our lives to serve his agenda and he will use every trick in his book to that end. But he will not prevail. Consider these words from Exodus 3:19-21: "But I am sure that the king of Egypt will not let you go, no, not even by a mighty hand. So

Favor the Elevator

I will stretch out My hand and strike Egypt with all My wonders which I will do in its midst; and after that he will let you go. And I will give this people favor in the sight of the Egyptians; and it shall be, when you go, that you shall not go empty-handed" (NKJV).

When favor speaks, it breaks the back of the enemy and God's people will not come out empty handed. God's people will come out in abundance. Proverbs 13:22 says, "A good man leaves an inheritance to his children's children, but the wealth of the sinner is stored up for the righteous" (NKJV). Through God's favor, the wealth transfer has begun!

Innovation

Chapter Eighteen
Honor Brings Favor

It is important for us to know why favor has been given. You can be assured that God's purpose for your life is always greater than money. Not long after Israel was delivered out of Egypt's hand, Moses went up to receive direction from God. He spent many days on the mountain hearing from God. In his absence, the people built a golden calf and began to worship it as their god. This was idolatry. Idolatry is defined as exalting anything above the Lord. The ironic thing is that when Moses was on the mountain, the Lord gave him this as a first command: "I am the Lord your God, who brought you out of the land of Egypt, out of the house of bondage." It is important to realize that in the absence of purpose, idolatry sets in. We can't allow our money to become a god; we must realize money is simply the fruit of favor.

Without the favor of God, the measure of blessing in our lives would not be the same. Sometimes people are envious of others because of where they live or where they work or what they have. But the truth is, God has given you favor for your own unique circumstances. Outside of that favor, you are not the same person and your level of productivity is greatly diminished.

The Israelites built an idol out of their wealth. God gave Israel wealth for a purpose. He did not give them wealth so they could go to the mall to go shopping or to a fancy restaurant. He allowed them to plunder the Egyptians and emerge from slavery with great wealth (Exodus 12:35-36) because He wanted them to build Him a place of worship where He could come and meet with them. God's plan has always been communion. He always desires to be the center of our lives and communities.

Ecclesiastes 5:19 tells us, "Every man also to whom God hath given riches and wealth, and hath given power to eat thereof and to take his portion and to rejoice in his labor, this is the gift of God" (KJV). This scripture tells us that God has given us riches and wealth as a gift. We must never deceive ourselves by thinking that what we have is a result of our own doing. It is given by Him and we need to worship Him with the things He has blessed us with.

Deuteronomy 8:18 says, "But thou shalt remember the LORD thy God: for it is he that giveth thee power to get wealth, that He may establish His covenant" (KJV). We are to reflect and understand this covenant in the way we live in the favor God has placed upon our lives. God had given Israel wealth so they could cross over and take possession of the Promised Land. Likewise, God has blessed us so that we can accomplish what He has called us to do and finance revival upon the earth. Our prayers to God should never be about making a certain income, but rather we should ask God to give us a certain amount of His kingdom. God will honor those prayers.

Favor is the affection of God towards you. Favor causes you to live under open heavens so that you can experience God's creativity and maneuver through every difficult situation life throws at you. The spirit of innovation is alive and well because we live in the favor of God as we follow Him in obedience.

In order for us to continue to live in favor by following in obedience, we have to learn how to empty ourselves of every thought that is not in harmony with God's truth. Consider this example of the early church found in Acts 2:46-47: "So continuing daily with one accord in the temple, and breaking bread from house to house, they ate their food with gladness and simplicity of heart, praising God and having favor with all the people" (NKJV).

Notice the order here. God gave them favor because they were praising God and living in one accord. Their position of worship and gratitude opened them up to receive favor, which caused supernatural increase to come into their lives. Honor brings favor. We need the favor of God to accomplish the things we have been assigned to do upon this planet. Favor causes us to defy the "worldly gravity" that constantly pulls us back from accomplishing God's will.

In Deuteronomy 6:1-3, God gives an exhortation to His people: "These are the commands, decrees and laws the LORD your God directed me to teach you to observe in the land that you are crossing the Jordan to possess, so that you, your children and their children after them may fear the LORD your God as long as you live by keeping all his decrees and commands that I give you, and so that you may enjoy long life. Hear, Israel, and be careful to obey so that it may go well with you and that you may increase greatly in a land flowing with milk and honey, just as the LORD, the God of your ancestors, promised you" (NIV).

Posession of the land of milk and honey was contingent upon God's people continuing to honor Him in the land. God told His people that as long as they observed His decrees and stayed within the boundaries of His word, they would receive favor. If they did not, then they would not experience His favor. In chemistry, one small change in the composition of a substance can make a drastic difference. For example, you know that water is comprised of two atoms of hydrogen and one atom of oxygen ($H_2 0$). But add one more atom of oxygen and you have H_2O_2, or hydrogen peroxide, which is a vastly different compound. One small deviation changes everything. That's what God was telling His people. If they stayed within the parameters He set, they would experience His favor. But one step outside those parameters and their experience would be vastly different. Isaiah 1:19 declares, "If ye be willing and obedient, ye shall eat the good of the land" (NKJV).

In understanding the principle that honor brings favor, we must first understand that our actions determine the divine reaction we experience. Consider the example of Jabez found in 1 Chronicles 4:9-10: "And Jabez was more honorable than his brethren: and his mother called his name Jabez [that is, Sorrowful], saying, Because I bare him with sorrow. And Jabez called on the God of Israel, saying, Oh that thou wouldest bless me indeed and enlarge my coast, and that thine hand might be with me and that thou wouldest keep me from evil, that it may not grieve me! And God granted him that which he requested" (KJV, explanation mine).

Jabez was able to request something larger than his current reality because he honored God. Jabez experienced much opposition in his life. Even his own mother saw no good in him, choosing instead to name him "Sorrow." But the favor of God broke the backbone of opposition in his life and it will do the same for us.

Another truth is that as we are faithful with the favor we are shown, we will experience more favor. We must be good stewards. The Bible tells us that if we cannot be faithful with a little, then how can we think God will trust us with more (Luke 16:10)? We must be faithful with the favor God has already shown us. Proverbs 3:9-10 teaches us, "Honor the LORD with thy substance and with the firstfruits of all thine increase: so shall thy barns be filled with plenty, and thy presses shall burst out with new wine" (KJV).

In 2 Kings 13:18-19, we see an interesting story that sheds light on another aspect of God's Spirit of innovation which brings us deliverance. Elisha the prophet was about to die when he was visited by King Jehoash, the reigning king of Israel. God had one more message for Elisha to deliver, which prompted this exchange: "Then he said, 'Take the arrows,' and the king took them. Elisha told him, 'Strike the ground.' He struck it three times and stopped. The man of God was angry with him and said, 'You should have struck the ground five or six times; then you would have defeated Aram and completely destroyed it. But now you will defeat it only three times'" (NIV).

Innovation

King Jehoash did not realize the unlimited victory that could have been his. The prophet Elisha was sent by God to make that plain to him. Visionaries affect our focus. God puts visionaries in our lives to make us aware of the great potential that lies within us. God never rewards a conservative spirit, but extends favor to the abundant thinker. If Jehoash had thought more abundantly, he could have destroyed his enemies once and for all. But instead, because of his small thinking, he destined himself to struggle. How many times do we fall short of God's plans for our lives because we make God small by our small visions?

If you are going to be a kingdom minded person, you have to reject smallmindedness and dream big. One rendering of the Greek word for favor (*karisse*) is to cause to find. One of the things that favor does in our life is cause us to find hidden potential on the inside. God's favor brings to light facts we previously knew nothing about, divine instructions and assignments that cause us to break through to be the kind of person God wants us to become.

Colossians 1:9 says, "And so, from the day we heard, we have not ceased to pray for you, asking that you may be filled with the knowledge of his will in all spiritual wisdom and understanding" (ESV). I pray that you are constantly coming into a greater awareness of the things that God has freely bestowed upon your life. His mercies are new every morning and His covenant love never fails. The greater knowledge we receive of His favor and love, the more effective we become in His kingdom. King Jehoash limited the scope of his victory because his knowledge of God was too small. Let us grow in our knowledge of God and honor

Him for all He has shown us that we may experience greater favor. Honor brings favor.

James 4:5-6 tells us, "Or do you think Scripture says without reason that he jealously longs for the spirit he has caused to dwell in us? But he gives us more grace. That is why Scripture says: 'God opposes the proud but shows favor to the humble'" (NIV). Humility opens us up to receive favor. Pride keeps us from the presence of God, but humility brings an injection of favor. We come into the presence of God through worship and honor of Him. We worship those who are above us in authority. As we show our deference to God through our worship, He honors us with His favor.

In the movie *Chariots of Fire*, the character Eric Lidell refused to run the 100 meter race because it was to take place on a Sunday. He was honoring the Lord's Sabbath. He did, however, run the 400 meter because the race took place on a Tuesday. He went on to set a world record in that event. The Lord spoke to Benny Hinn and told him he needed to obtain favor with the arch bishop before he spoke in a particular country. Hinn obeyed and sought the favor of his superior as God directed, and God opened up the country for a fruitful ministry. Thousands came to Christ.

In Judges 6:2-4, we see the plight of the Israelites under Midianite oppression: "And the hand of Midian prevailed against Israel; and because of the Midianites the children of Israel made for themselves the dens which are in the mountains and caves and strongholds. And so it was, when Israel had sown, that the Midianites came up, and the Amalekites, and the children of the East, even they came up against them. And they encamped against

Innovation

them and destroyed the increase of the earth till thou come unto Gaza, and left no sustenance for Israel, neither sheep, nor ox, nor ass" (KJV). The Midianites were destroying the harvest that God had intended for His people. Thankfully, that is not the end of the story. Israel turned the cried out to God and God sent them a deliverer – Gideon.

Gideon may not have been the obvious choice of deliverer, but He was God's man for that time. When the angel first appeared to Gideon, Gideon was hiding from the Midianites, threshing his wheat in a winepress. When the angel told Gideon that he would be the answer to the Israelites cries for deliverance, Gideon was frightened at first. But what do we see him do? In Judges 6:19, we see that Gideon honored the angel with a gift. The ritual of honor overrode Gideon's trepidation. The Bible says in verse 24 that this place where the angel met with Gideon came to be known as Jehovah Shalom. This became a place of peace. God can turn a land of poverty, a land of trepidation, into a place of peace when we choose to honor the Lord through our giving, our worship, and our hearts of humility.

Gideon initially had great fear. The word "fear" comes from the word *phobos*, which means intimidation of adversities. Never forget that fear tolerated is faith contaminated. God had to give Gideon a revelation that he was a mighty man of valor. In the light of God's favor, that is who he was. He needed to see himself in the light of God's favor if he was to rise up and conquer. Honoring God's angel helped him see what he could be in the light of God's favor. When the enemy tries to steal your harvest and destroy the thing you've labored for, honor will cause you to rise to the top again.

The great author Nathaniel Hawthorne came home one day, heartbroken because he had lost his job. Hawthorne's wife's response to the news that her husband had lost their sole source of income was incredible. She simply said, "Now you can write that book you want to write."

Hawthorne responded to her comment with the obvious question, "What are we going to live on?"

His wife pulled out a large sum of money that she had been saving. She honored her husband when she told him, "I always knew you were a genius and that one day you would write a great masterpiece." Hawthorn began to write and today, almost every library in America has a copy of his work, *The Scarlet Letter*, on their shelves.

When we honor, it releases greatness. When we honor, it releases innovation. It releases the creativity necessary to do what we were put on earth to do. If your brook has dried up, create a new stream. Act with honor. Call on God's favor. Release His creativity. Live in the innovative dimension through His power.

Innovation

Honor Brings Favor

BILL AND ANNE

Dr. Bill holds doctorate degrees in Theology and Philosophy of Christian Education and has been in pastoral and evangelistic ministry since 1981. In 1985, he married his wife, Anne - who holds a masters degree in Education as well as a doctorate degree in Ministry - and together, they joined forces in the ministry. Bill and Anne have a unique style of ministry that inspires and encourages you to live life in a supernatural way. After planting several churches and doing extensive ministry work, they founded Livingway Family Church - a growing multi-campus church in Brownsville, Texas - where they have served as pastors ever since. Bill and Anne have three children: Christopher, Marcus and Ryan, whose family includes wife Jacquelyn and son Harper. Bill and Anne have also authored three books: *Show Us the Father*, *Discover Your Assignment*, and *Fearonomics*. In addition to pastoring, Bill and Anne travel internationally, speaking with an emphasis on equipping leaders and pastors to reach both their communities and their world.

PRAYER OF SALVATION

God loves you—no matter who you are, no matter what your past. God loves you so much that He gave His one and only begotten Son for you. The Bible tells us that "...whoever believes in Him shall not perish but have eternal life" (John 3:16 NIV). Jesus laid down His life and rose again so that we could spend eternity with Him in heaven and experience His absolute best on earth. If you would like to receive Jesus into your life, say the following prayer out loud and mean it from your heart.

Heavenly Father, I come to You admitting that I am a sinner. Right now, I choose to turn away from sin, and I ask You to cleanse me of all unrighteousness. I believe that Your Son, Jesus, died on the cross to take away my sins. I also believe that He rose again from the dead so that I might be forgiven of my sins and made righteous through faith in Him. I call upon the name of Jesus Christ to be the Savior and Lord of my life. Jesus, I choose to follow You and ask that You fill me with the power of the Holy Spirit. I declare that right now I am a child of God. I am free from sin and full of the righteousness of God. I am saved in Jesus' name. Amen.

If you prayed this prayer to receive Jesus Christ as your Savior for the first time, please contact us on the Web at **www.harrisonhouse.com** to receive a free book.

Or you may write to us at
Harrison House • P.O. Box 35035 • Tulsa, Oklahoma 74153

The Harrison House Vision

Proclaiming the truth and the power

Of the Gospel of Jesus Christ

With excellence;

Challenging Christians to

Live victoriously,

Grow spiritually,

Know God intimately.